Isolation

A Place of Transformation in the Life of a Leader

Isolation

A Place of Transformation in the Life of a Leader

Shelley G. Trebesch

BARNABAS PUBLISHERS

Altadena, California

Barnabas Publishers
P.O. Box 6006
Altadena CA 91003-6006

Printed in the United States of America

ISBN 0974181846

FORWARD

All leaders face deep processing at some time in their lives. Many do so more than once. Deep processing refers to those activities that God uses to force a leader to seriously evaluate life and ministry. God uses such activities as isolation, conflict, and life crises (health or otherwise) to deepen a leader's relationship with God, to create a sense of utter dependence upon God, and to build foundational leadership character qualities in their life. From this kind of shaping activity, superintended by God, comes an important by-product: spiritual authority[†].

In my opinion, we are better prepared to cooperate with God in this deep processing when we understand as much as we can about it. We can life schedule, that is, expect it, gird our wills for it, and move with God through it. To do this, we identify it in our lives when it comes and recognize the responses God wants from us and His purposes in it. In other words, "Forewarned is forearmed!" Getting perspective on what happens in deep processing is a major step forward in our seeing God's benefits in it.

I have seen two basic reactions of leaders to isolation processing. One, some respond by saying if this is the way God is, I will have no more to do with Him. And so they reject the deep processing and its attendant benefits and even God and perhaps the Christian way. Two, many respond by going deep with God in the shaping activity. They come out on the other side as leaders who have found the comfort of Christ in the situation and can now minister that same comfort to others (2 Corinthians 1:3,4).

I have known Shelley Trebesch for almost five years in a mentoring relationship. I have seen her share these insights with leaders at workshops, seminars and classes. I have watched her as she herself has gone through deep processing. She is our resident expert on isolation processing in particular and deep processing in general. She has experienced what she writes about. She is a 2nd Corinthians person.[§] Read carefully her insights. You will sooner or later need them for your own life, either in prospect or retrospect. And you will most certainly need them to help leaders around you develop.

Dr. J. Robert Clinton
June 1996

[†] Spiritual authority is an ideal power base that a leader employs with followers to influence them toward God's purposes for them. Spiritual authority is the right to influence conferred upon a leader by followers because of their perception of spirituality in that leader. It is that characteristic of a God-anointed leader, which is developed upon an experiential power base that enables him/her to influence followers through: 1. Persuasion, 2. Force of modeling, and 3. Moral expertise. Spiritual authority comes to a leader in three major ways. As leaders go through deep experiences with God they experience the sufficiency of God to meet them in those situations. They come to know God. This experiential knowledge of God and the deep experiences with God are part of the experiential acquisition of spiritual authority. And that is what we are talking about in this book. A second way that spiritual authority comes is through a life which models godliness. When the Spirit of God is transforming a life into the image of Christ those characteristics of love, joy, peace, long suffering, gentleness, goodness, faith, meekness, and temperance carry great weight in giving credibility that the leader is consistent inward and outward. A third way that spiritual authority comes is through giftedpower. When a leader can demonstrate in ministry gifted power—that is, a clear testimony to divine intervention in the ministry—there will be spiritual authority. Now while all three of these ways of getting spiritual authority should be a part of a leader, it is frequently the case that one or more of the elements dominates.

[§] A 2nd Corinians person, like Paul, is one who has been through deep processing experiences and has learned about power in weakness and God's revealing Himself through clay pots. Such a person knows about spiritual authority.

ABSTRACT

For various reasons, leaders experience several critical periods in which they are set apart from full-time ministry. We call these periods "isolation experiences." And despite the pain that often ensues during an isolation time, these times are crucial for the development of a leader. God's shaping activities in isolation times cause a leader to seriously evaluate his/her life and ministry and relationship to God. One who responds to God in isolation processing is a different person afterwards, living life more maturely and ministering out of being.

Embracing the isolation time is paramount to successfully negotiating this difficult period. Therefore, in this paper I endeavor to bring perspective for those in isolation and to those who will experience isolation by first giving an overview of biblical examples of those in isolation and then by exploring the process and results of a season of isolation. I then suggest steps one can take toward development while in isolation.

I give a number of cases, some biblical and some historical and even a few contemporary. These cases will help you feel some of the emotions of isolation processing as well as illustrate some of the processes I describe.

Essentially there are two types of isolation experiences in terms of entry—involuntary and voluntary. In either case the leader experiences four processes—stripping, wrestling with God, increased intimacy with God, and release for the future. Just knowing these processes helps ease one's confusion in isolation processing.

Three wonderful things result from isolation processing. A leader experiences transformation in his/her inner-life. There is a sensed spiritual transformation. And there is progress in ministerial formation. All three of these formational results will integrate to focus the leader more appropriately for the being and doing side of ministry.

I have found Psalm 42 to be wonderfully suggestive as to how to heighten one's development in isolation. So I close this paper with six suggestions from Psalm 42 for getting the most you can out of God's time for you in isolation. Just the six topics alone are encouraging: Be Honest, Remember, Have Hope—Keep Perspective, Get a Mentor, Listen for the Voice of God, and embrace isolation.

Methodologically, the research for this paper was done primarily by comparative study and drawing conclusions from my own personal ministry experiences, from many case studies—including Biblical, historical, and contemporary—and personal interviews.

Over the past several years I have been greatly blessed as I have watched God use these insights with several emerging leaders. My ministry position puts me in contact on a personal level with mid-career students. Many of these are in the shock of an isolation time. With a number of these I have enjoyed a mentoring relationship. It has been gratifying to see God use these insights to help these leaders negotiate well, that is, embrace the isolation experience and greatly profit from it. May you find them as helpful!

Shelley Trebesch

TABLE OF CONTENTS

Introduction

I will use three case studies to introduce us to the notion of isolation processing. One is my own. Two come from the life of one of my favorite historical mentors—Amy Carmichael. I think you will gather just how important isolation experiences can be for God to get the attention of a leader.

Case Study A. Personal Experience After Five Years of Intense Campus Ministry

Upon first coming to Fuller Theological Seminary for a sabbatical I could not have been happier. After five years of intense ministry with InterVarsity Christian Fellowship in Arizona, I was ready to study, to reflect on my experiences and to meet God in my new schedule free of full-time ministry—a break from speaking engagements and training leaders and late night phone calls. I looked forward to many long hours of praying and listening to God and rejoicing in reflection on the fruitful years of ministry I had just experienced. I was hungry for God and could not wait to get more of him in my life. Those first months were blissful as I journaled, took retreats of silence at a local monastery and felt the affirming presence of God in my life. I had chosen to set myself apart from ministry for the sake of renewal in my life.

This blissful state was not to last long, however, and within six months of arriving at Fuller, I began to experience something entirely different than the "affirming presence" of God. I became sad and depressed. I did not seem to hear from God anymore. Gone were the days of his sweet presence. Gone were the days of hearing his confident voice speaking to me. I was experiencing a dark night of the soul, and I could not do anything to relieve the emotional and spiritual pain it caused. Not only did I experience an internal struggle, but my external world was falling a part as well. After six years of seeing God's faithfulness in meeting my financial needs, I ran out of money and needed to find a job—the sabbatical was over. The position I accepted as a small business manager in West Los Angeles further isolated me from the Fuller community and my support network. The pain increased. I asked deep questions such as "Will I ever do ministry again? Will I ever make a significant contribution to the Kingdom of God? Will I always be alone and filled with this much pain? Will I ever be in a job that is fulfilling?" and more crucially, "Why aren't you answering me, God? Will I ever hear your voice again?" Many mornings I wept at the thought of walking through the day's pain.[1]

Commentary on Case Study A

Perhaps you heard echoes of your own cries and felt similar feelings as you read the above description of a very dark period in my life. If so, perhaps you are in or have been in a similar silent, dark time. These times in the pilgrimage of the Christian have commonly been described as "dark nights of the soul" or "wilderness/desert" experiences. I elect to call

---

[1] Later, of course, there was the breakthrough and realization of God's presence and training through the time. But here I want to emphasize the affective side of entering into isolation. Many leaders will feel this same kind of pain that I am describing when they become isolated from ministry.

them "isolation experiences"[2] because this phrase further sheds light on the feelings during these experiences. They are the times when nothing satisfies the hunger in our souls. They are times when we try to run and escape the pain, but the pain hounds our every move. While we cringe at even the thought of such experiences, the Bible reveals them as a natural part of the life of faith. So prevalent are these desert times that they can be found in many lives of the leaders of the Bible. From the Scriptures we can see that these isolation or desert times always influence and have an impact on ministry and missions.

Therefore, I have chosen to explore this process in a leader's life. I will exegete several experiences of those in isolation. I will demonstrate the results of these times in their lives and draw from these results implications for life and ministry. You will notice that all the scenarios explored contain similar elements. Yet they, along with the resulting examples of transformation, will contribute something unique to our understanding of the process of isolation. Finally, I will exegete the process of isolation, as well as demonstrate how one can embrace and get everything God intends one to have as a result of a period of isolation.[3]

---

[2] Later I will define isolation more formally. But here you can catch the sense of it—especially being set aside from ministry and being driven into a deeper relationship with God. Some isolation experiences are deeper than others. St. John of the Cross uses the term "Dark Night of the Soul" to describe an isolation experience in which God can not be found. There is no felt presence of God. Some use the term "Desert Experience" to show how dry the time can be. I use the term isolation to point out that such an experience isolates one from ministry which is the usual way one gets affirmation. Since affirmation can not come in an isolation experience from achievement it must come through beingness. It is this drawing out of one's beingness that is a paradigm shift that most leaders used to plaudits from achievement struggle with in isolation.

[3] This is a recurring theme in all deep processing. Rather than wanting to get out of the time—that is get through the time fast, the normal attitude, you should instead endeavor to get out of the time, that is learn from it, all that God has for you in the time.

Case Study B. Amy Carmichael Early Isolation Experience

It seemed that the Lord blessed and multiplied everything she put her hand to; whether it be in the boroughs of England or in the vast land of India—Amy Carmichael[4] experienced the powerful presence and anointing of God in her life. Those around her witnessed the results. Yet, at several key junctures in her ministry, the Lord allowed her to be set aside for periods of isolation. These times were not her choice—she entered them all involuntarily either through sickness or accidents, but God used the periods to transform Carmichael into his image.[5]

Toward the end of 1890, Carmichael had established a thriving ministry through an outreach she had initiated for girls working in the factories of Manchester. Through her witness, many had come to know Christ, and therefore, Carmichael started Bible studies to train these young women. Because of her unending ministry, Carmichael became sick.[6] Although she tried to continue meeting with the girls and holding evangelistic campaigns, she was soon unable to continue the work. Carmichael's friend and spiritual mentor,[7] Robert Wilson, invited her to take a break and stay with him in Broughton-Grange. She was very reluctant, but finally gave in to his wisdom; unbeknownst to her at the time, she would

---

[4] Amy Carmichael was a brilliant missionary to India from 1895 to 1951. When she left the soil of England in 1895, she never returned but devoted herself wholly to ministry in her beloved India. She founded Dohnavur Fellowship initially to provide a home for the children she rescued from Hindu temple service (basically slave labor and prostitution). The community eventually housed over 140 boys and girls and Carmichael built a hospital in the compound as well.

[5] Thus far in the two cases given you see something of what I meant when I stated earlier that "For various reasons," leaders experience several critical periods in which they are set apart from full-time ministry. I entered my time of isolation voluntarily. I chose to leave ministry for a time of study. Amy Carmichael illustrates two other causes or reasons for entering isolation—sickness or accidents. The two general categories covering these types include voluntary and involuntary. As you can imagine involuntary carries with it at first the greater shock of being in isolation.

[6] This is probably a kind way of saying she had workaholic tendencies. She gave herself intensely to ministry.

need to take a very long break from ministry (Reid and Van Dalen, 1985: 32).

Carmichael ended up staying with Wilson for three years recovering from her illness. While she yearned to return to ministry and especially to continue her preparations for the mission field, she rested long enough to recover, but more importantly, long enough to embrace the treasure the Lord had in mind for this isolation period.

While she rested, Carmichael read classic authors such as Hudson Taylor and F. B. Meyer. She also steeped herself in theology. More importantly, she grew in her love for Scripture and prayer. Consequently, the years in Broughton-Grange were foundational for Carmichael's spiritual formation. Not only did she learn lessons from historical mentors, she also began to know God's voice as intimacy in her relationship with the Lord increased. Because of this time, she embraced God wholly even in those moments or periods when he seemed far away. This spiritual formation through isolation comforted and stabilized her relationship with the Lord as she left for the mission field immediately following the isolation experience.

Commentary on Case B.

This early isolation experience showed Amy Carmichael the importance of beingness— that is, her relationship with God. Up until this time she was a hard working young achiever. During this period of time she was introduced to "Deeper Life" truth by many of the Keswick speakers whom she got to know

---

[7] Mentoring is a relational experience in which one person who knows something, the mentor, transfers that something (the power resources such as wisdom, advice, information emotional support, protection, linking to resources, career guidance, status) to someone else, the mentoree. There are several ways in which mentors work with mentorees. See Clinton and Clinton, 1992, The Mentor Handbook, published by Barnabas Publishers. In this case Wilson served as a spirituality mentor, a contemporary model, a counselor, a teacher, and a sponsor. This was a time of great transformation in Amy Carmichael's life.

through Robert Wilson. She learned the importance of rest and recovery. The time period was three years in isolation. While she was initially propelled into it because of sickness, she later chose to remain in it because of what she was getting out of it.

Case Study C. Carmichael—Later Isolation Experience; Renewal Through Pain

In some ways Carmichael began and ended her life of ministry in isolation. Carmichael saw 30 years of incredible fruitfulness in her ministry in India. She rescued many children from the bondage of temple servitude; she established a community and school in which they could belong; she challenged and trained many leaders to join her in ministering to the forgotten; she fought the enemy for the very lives of many innocent victims. It could be said that Carmichael's heart was the very heart of Jesus, she was filled with so much compassion.

Aside from ministry accomplishments, Carmichael also demonstrated a discerning missiological approach toward the ministry. In a class of her own for the time period, Carmichael wrestled with how to contextualize the gospel and worship for Indian believers. As a result, she established innovative services which matched the heart of the Indian people. Yet, in the midst of convergence and in the midst of a very fruitful ministry, Carmichael entered another season of isolation and this season took her to her death in 1951.[8]

Carmichael seemed to have an "inner readiness for all of life's unexpected calls." (Reid and Van Dalen, 1985) So, when she fell into a pit and severely broke her leg and ankle, she

---

[8] While most isolations periods are relatively short, 3 months to 2 or 3 years, occasionally you will see an extended isolation time. In extended times, the isolation decreases in intensity of isolation lessons and the person will usually accommodate to the new situation and learn to minister out of that situation but usually in new ways.

embraced her new situation with grace. The leg did not heal properly, however, (she suffered excruciating pain almost daily) so her injury, combined with other physical ailments, confined her mostly to her room for the next 20 years of her life. Was her ministry over?

Even the intensely faithful Carmichael asked this question and felt concerned over who would take over the leadership of Dohnavur Fellowship. She prayed continually for physical healing so that she could return to her ministry, but in 1933, the Lord spoke a firm "no" to this request (Reid and Van Dalen, 1985: 67). In absence of healing, the Lord did begin to reveal his purposes for this isolation period. Carmichael caught a glimpse in a line of a poem by Henry Vaughn— "O let me climb when I lye down." (as quoted in Houghton, 1953: 297) Carmichael was beginning a more intense, intimate transformation toward being like Christ.

Some of Carmichael's most important break-throughs in writing and in her relationship with the Lord came during these 20 years of isolation. She wrote 13 books and many songs in her hours alone. She also published the "Dust of Gold Newsletter," which was read all over the world. In fact, this newsletter had a profound influence on many young people and acted to mobilize many for missions. It also told the truth about the spiritual reality of India which heightened people's consciousness for the marginalized.[9] More importantly to Carmichael, however, was her growth in intimacy with the Lord.

During this isolation period, Carmichael's relationship with the Lord reached a profound depth. She listened for his voice and heard his whisper. She spoke quietly and saw him move through her prayers. She reached out her hands to him and he affirmed her life. In this sweet fulfillment of her relationship with Jesus—as a result of a season of isolation—Car-

---

[9] Those who are basically powerless in society and who suffer in terms of poverty, social acceptance, job opportunities, discrimination and opportunities for a better way of life.

michael went to meet her Lord face-to-face in 1951 having never really entered active ministry again.

Commentary on Case Study C

Probably the most important thing to learn from this latter experience is that God uses isolation experiences to accomplish things through us that we could never accomplish apart from the isolation experience. And isolation experiences can come late in life as well as early in life or in mid-career. Sometimes some of our ultimate contributions may come from an isolation time.[10]

Summary

Isolation experiences can be painful. They most certainly will be profitable when we recognize God's working through them. They can last a relatively short time or be extended. When we talk about isolation proper we are talking about a variable time from 3 months to 3 or 4 years. When we talk about an extended isolation time it could last for a very long time but with varying intensity, more intense at first and less as time goes on. We must, no matter how long it takes, get the value out of isolation that God has in it. Lets move on now to define more carefully what we have just been introduced to. I'll begin with a word picture and then move on to a word definition.

---

[10] See Clinton 1989 paper, The Ultimate Contribution, which analyzes categories of legacies left behind by effective leaders. Twelve types are identified. One type is writings. Here Carmichael poured out her life and

DEFINING ISOLATION

Picture Definition—Wilderness, Desert

The dictionary defines the words "wilderness" and "desert" as regions of "uncultivated" and "uninhabited" land (Webster's 1981: 1331, 305). They are lonely, desolate areas where there are few, if any, human beings. The Hebrew word (*midar*) is translated as both wilderness and desert, and likewise, the Greek word (*eramous*) is translated wilderness and desert depending on the particular geographical region being referenced (Brown et al. 1979: 184 & Bauer, Gingrich and Danker 1979: 309). With the exception of several figurative instances, most occurrences of these words in the text refer to an actual region of land. Yet, over the many centuries of Christian spirituality, words such as "desert" and "wilderness" have been used to describe one's spiritual condition.

During a desert or wilderness time, one is removed from his/her normal, daily routine or home and isolated from friends and family. A person in a desert time may not feel the presence of God, and it may seem that he/she is alone in a dark and foreign land. One cannot rely on what used to be familiar. The person consequently walks through a breaking or stripping process after which his/her character becomes transformed.

As it relates to leaders, Clinton labels such a process as "isolation processing" and defines it as:

Leadership Development Definition

Isolation is the setting aside of a leader from normal ministry involvement in its natural context usually for an extended time in order to experience God in a new or deeper way (Clinton 1989: 274).

By observing case studies of leaders' lives, quasi isolation experiences have been found as well.

Quasi-isolation definition: Ministry Isolation

Ministry isolation is an experience in the context of ministry in which the basic symptoms of regular isolation are felt and experienced and in which God uses the situation to deepen the leader's life.

Leaders often experience quasi-isolation in ministry. These experiences can occur when leaders go through a paradigm shift[11]. Paradigm shifts change the way people view a particular situation by changing the worldview orientation of the person. If a leader in an organization experiences a paradigm shift when no one else does, this paradigm shift may propel the leader into an isolation experience. Paradigm shifts change the way a leader does ministry. If she is the only one in a group who has experienced the shift, she may experience the processing of isolation—thus, a quasi-isolation experience because she is still in ministry. There is that sense of separation due to the different experience.

---

[11] A paradigm shift is a major shaping activity used by God to give breakthroughs in a leader's life. It is a major change in perspective that revolutionizes how a leader sees something. See Clinton's 1993 paper on this, The Paradigm Shift—God's Way of Opening New Vistas to Leaders. Available through Barnabas Publishers, P.O. Box 6006, Altadena, CA, 91003-6006.

Quasi-isolation can also occur when leaders experience some type of transforming event, such as getting psychotherapy. Leaders experience the transformation, but others on their team may not have experienced the transformation. This too can lead to isolation processing. There is a sense of one being different or separated from the others due to a different life changing event.

Isolation Examples
In The Old Testament

Case D. Joseph, An Unjust Wilderness Adventure

Joseph experiences two distinctly different isolation experiences. The first, Joseph's wilderness experience, begins in Genesis chapter 37 when his jealous brothers sell him into slavery. Joseph's brothers resented him for being the favored child of his father Jacob. From the account, we also know that Joseph himself has contributed to their resentment by arrogantly telling them two dreams in which he rises up and rules over them. Thus, in chapter 39 we find Joseph in Egypt having been sold to Potiphar, one of Pharaoh' s officials. Potiphar's wife tries to seduce Joseph, but Joseph maintains his integrity and refuses her repeated advances, declaring that he would not sin against God. She, however, continues to pursue him, and one time actually grabs his cloak and keeps it to show her husband when he returns. The wife tells Potiphar that Joseph has initiated the advance and therefore, Potiphar has Joseph imprisoned. Joseph then enters his second isolation experience.

Case E. Joseph, Prison Isolation

One can imagine the feelings Joseph must have experienced during this ordeal, having twice been betrayed. Joseph did not choose these circumstances, and now he sits alone in prison. Where is God in all of this isolation and hardship?

The Bible makes it very clear (Gen. 39: 2, 3, 21, and 23) that the LORD was with Joseph and gave him success in everything he did. Those around Joseph—Potiphar, the prison guards and finally even Pharaoh—recognize this and continually promote Joseph to some type of leadership position, even while a slave and prisoner. Eventually God sovereignly places Joseph as the chief minister in Pharaoh's kingdom, second only to Pharaoh, by giving Joseph an interpretation for Pharaoh's dreams.

Commentary on Joseph's Isolation Experiences

In some sense Joseph brought on his isolation experience. His special relationship with his father so angered his brothers that they were willing to get rid of him. And yet God was even in that, protecting him and coincidently providing a way to get him to Egypt, the place where Joseph will fulfill his destiny.

We know that these intense wilderness or isolation experiences develop in Joseph a depth of maturity, which in turn places him in a position to be used by God. The young Joseph who arrogantly told his brothers, mother and father that he would rule over them has become a humble servant of the LORD who attributes all of his success and gifts to the LORD. For example, when Joseph interprets Pharaoh's dreams, he flatly tells the Pharaoh that it is not himself that gives the interpretation, but rather God. In Joseph's isolation, a profound trust as well as relationship with God seems to have been developed. He trusts God to act on his behalf and he hears the LORD's leading as he acts. Baldwin says this isolation experience is designed to put "steel into faith" so Joseph's faith becomes mature (Baldwin 1986: 171).

Key Points from Joseph's Isolation Experiences

The following observations can prove helpful to those of us who are unjustly placed into isolation:

- Seasons of isolation bring character transformation.
- God can use a season of isolation to break a leader's arrogance and self-confidence. Such a breaking process can also restore a leader to become what God really created that leader to be.
- God stays with a leader in isolation even if circumstances appear just the opposite. During this time, the leader's trust in God deepens.
- Seeds of destiny (Joseph's dreams) point the way to the future, but leaders cannot force their destiny to happen.
- God often uses isolation experiences to position a leader for the next phase of ministry. Both isolation experiences were necessary for Joseph to be where God could network him to the place and position from which his destiny could be fulfilled.

Case F. Moses, Isolation on the Run

Moses enters a wilderness time in a different way than Joseph. Having been raised in Pharaoh's household by Pharaoh's daughter (Exodus 2), Moses has known privilege, the finest education and royal training (LaSor, Hubbard, and Bush 1982: 132). Aware of his Hebrew heritage, however, Moses empathizes with the plight of his fellow Hebrews who are oppressed slaves of the Egyptian government. One day Moses witnesses the brutality of one of the Egyptian foremen toward a Hebrew slave and takes the matter into his own hands, killing the Egyptian. Moses' crime becomes known, and he flees to the desert of Midian. There he joins Jethro's family and marries one of his daughters. Not only is Moses cut off from his Hebrew heritage, but he is also cut off from the culture he has been raised in, the Egyptian culture. Everything he has known—power, prestige and privilege—evaporated in his rash act of killing an Egyptian, and now he finds himself in an alien land with an alien wife and shepherding sheep. In just one incident Moses goes from being a man groomed to be a government official to being a man on the run who becomes a simple, hard-working shepherd.

We are not certain how long Moses remained in Midian cut off from his people. It was long enough to become fairly well established in Midian with Jethro's family and long enough to have a son. However, Moses does not forget his past failure, for when God eventually appears to him in the burning bush (Ex. 3) and calls him to be his instrument for delivering the Israelites from the Egyptians, Moses tries to refuse this leadership assignment several times stating, "Who am I that I should go to Pharaoh and bring the Israelites out of Egypt?" (Ex. 3:11). In his broken state, Moses questions God many times regarding the call the Lord is placing on his life. God patiently answers all of Moses' questions and even gives him a partner for ministry, his brother Aaron.

Thus, as Moses embraces the call on his life, we discover a transformed Moses—from one who confidently took matters into his own hands to a reluctant leader who learns how to trust God. The transformed Moses is described as "a very humble man, more humble than anyone else on the face of the earth" and one who speaks to God "face to face" (Num. 12: 3, 8). He certainly wasn't this way before he left Egypt.

Commentary on Moses' Extended Isolation Experience

Moses was set aside from his life purpose for a very long period of time. At first the isolation was intense as he went through the shock of adjusting to a different language, lifestyle, and loss of privilege. But eventually the extended isolation away from family, culture, and position lessened as the new way of life was embraced. During this time God worked on his character as seen by his response at the burning bush.

Key Points from Moses' Isolation Experience

• Character transformation occurs in seasons of isolation. God creates a posture of humbleness in the lives of leaders during isolation.
• Isolation can happen in preparation for ministry.
• Leaders use the lessons learned in isolation for future ministry. Moses learned how to simply care for livestock and his family in the wilderness of Midian. This knowledge served him later when he led the Israelites in the desert.
• Increased intimacy with God is the primary fruit of an isolation experience.

Case G. Elijah, Unexpected Preparation for Ministry

Perhaps the most memorable highlight of Elijah's ministry is his confrontation with the Baal prophets on Mount Carmel. What prepares Elijah for such an encounter? What has happened in Elijah's relationship with God that Elijah trusts God so explicitly? How does Elijah hear the Lord so clearly? Interestingly, in the story previous to the Mt. Carmel confrontation, Elijah is not in the temple receiving training nor is he sitting at the feet of a famous rabbi. Rather, Elijah is in the school of isolation, in the wilderness.

Elijah's wilderness experience begins three years previous to the encounter on Mount Carmel. After making the pronouncement to King Ahab that there will be drought in the land, Elijah immediately leaves for the wilderness on the east side of the Jordan (I Kings 17). Elijah is alone for a long period of time, and he drinks from a brook and is fed by ravens. Each day he has to trust God to send ravens to bring meat and bread to eat. After some time, the brook dries up, and the Lord speaks to Elijah, telling him to go to Zarephath of Sidon (further east, further away from Israel, further into isolation).[12] Elijah stays there for three years in the home of a widow and

---

[12] This points out the repeated observation in many leaders' experience. Success in ministry brings problems. This will be repeated with Elijah's great success on Mount Carmel. He runs for his life.

her son. God speaks to Elijah telling him that this widow will supply him with food. However, when Elijah meets the widow, she is almost out of flour and oil and is preparing to make the last meal before dying. Elijah asks her to make him some food saying "this is what the LORD, the God of Israel, says: 'The jar of flour will not be used up and the jug of oil will not run dry until the day the LORD gives rain on the land.'" (I King 17:14) So, for three years the widow and Elijah trust God for their food and for three years the Lord provides their daily needs for food.

Upon first interacting with this passage, it may seem like a waste of time for Elijah to spend three years with this widow in a foreign land. Shouldn't he be prophesying to the people of Israel? Shouldn't he be trying to turn an evil king from his evil ways so the people would follow God once again?

Yet, God very sovereignly led Elijah to Zarephath and kept him there for three years. We know that Elijah's dependence upon the Lord must have grown during this time. Each day he witnessed the miracle of God's provision as the supply of flour and oil never ended. This type of dependence and the demonstration of God's faithfulness formed in Elijah a trust in God that would carry him on to trust God in the power encounter with the prophets of Baal. So profound was his trust in God that he very deliberately made his sacrifice impossible to burn in order to demonstrate God's power (I Kings 18:30-35). In the end, God demonstrates his sovereignty and power by consuming the sacrifice with fire. The Baal prophets are shamed and eventually killed. Elijah's three years in the kiln of trust development enabled him to be used as a powerful vessel of God.

Case H. Elijah, Success Brings Problems

A second shorter isolation experience surprised Elijah. Following Elijah's great triumph on Mount Carmel he flees for his life. God protects him. This was a desert isolation experience both literally and figuratively. Though relatively short, this intensive isolation experience powerfully affects Elijah. Elijah has despaired and lost hope. He even contemplates suicide. But an angel touches him. And in the cave on Mount Horeb Elijah learns some important lessons for his life. One of the major isolation feelings is pinpointed in this isolation experience. Elijah has a strong sense of personal rejection. Accompanying this is the sense that he is alone in standing up for God (and receiving the backlash). But God does two things here. He corrects Elijah's view. No, there are 7000 who have not bowed the knee. And God graces Elijah with a sense of his presence. And note the methodology. A quiet inner voice. Elijah went on after this experience to mentor Elisha.

Key Points from Elijah's Isolation Experience

- God sets up isolation experiences to form dependence and trust in leaders.
- Leaders of God must trust God explicitly in the small things of faith so they can explicitly trust God in the large things of faith.
- Isolation experiences are never a waste of time.
- What may seem like meaningless, unproductive service may in fact contain the most profound leadership and spiritual lessons.
- After great victories expect downers including the possibility of a mini-isolation experience.
- A major symptom of isolation is frequently the sense of personal rejection.

Case I. The Israelites, Typifying the Wilderness Experience

In many regards the Israelites' wanderings in the desert typify a wilderness experience. In fact, after the exodus, their wilderness experience became a symbol to the Jews of God's guidance and providence in contrast to humankind's rebellion (Douglas ed., et al. 1982: 1253). In the beginning of the exodus out of Egypt, God used the desert as a place to regroup and regather his people—a place to once again establish the Israelite cultural identity and worship of him as their God. Yet, as the Israelites rebelled, the desert became a place of punishment resulting from their disobedience until finally, one whole generation passed away while in the desert (Num. 14). Therefore, unlike the other desert experiences we have explored so far, God may send one into or keep one in the desert because of disobedience.

The Israelite desert experience included the dependence theme as well. The Israelites received their guidance and their food from the hand of God. They were totally dependent on God for food each day which he provided in the dew of manna. They also looked to him for water and on several occasions the Lord brought the water out of a dry, hard rock. On the whole, the Israelite's wandering in the desert took on a type of testing and response pattern with the ultimate goal being that the Israelites would trust God, that they would be his people and that he would be their God. [13]

Thus, we see that wilderness experiences can contain a type of test with the hoped for result that the servant or servants of God will trust God. It must be said that God always remains faithful in these scenarios; however, humans do not always remain faithful to God. What is sobering about the Israelites' wilderness experience is that some did not come out of the wilderness—some did not pass the test and cling to God. The unfaithful generation ultimately does not see the fruit of the desert and enter the promise land. When in the desert, one must continue to trust and relate to God—clinging to him as the only hope for life.

---

[13] The testing/response pattern occurs over and over again in the lives of leaders. A situation arises in which the leader has a choice of whether to respond positively in faith or negatively in disbelief or rebellion. If the response is negative, it is likely that the leader will come across this situation later on in life and have the opportunity to respond positively again.

Key Points from the Israelites' Isolation Experience

- Isolation experiences form trust in and dependence on the Lord.
- Isolation is designed to bring intimancy with and deep worship of God.
- Isolation may be God's intentional plan because of the disobedience of his people.

ISOLATION EXAMPLES IN THE NEW TESTAMENT

We find wilderness/isolation experiences in the New Testament as well although the examples are not as prolific. I explore two such experiences in the sections below—Jesus and Paul. It must be stated from the beginning, however, that Jesus' wilderness experience was not designed for his own personal transformation, but for the transformation of people's understanding of the ministry of the Messiah.

Case J. Jesus, Identifying with Our Wilderness Experiences

Kraybill insightfully points out that the number "forty" in the Israelite history represents trial or testing, the most obvious instance being the Hebrews wandering in the desert (Kraybill 1978: 41). With this in mind, we now exegete Jesus' forty days of testing in the wilderness using the gospel of Luke.

John baptizes Jesus in the Jordan, and the Spirit leads Jesus out into the wilderness. Here Jesus fasts for forty days and eventually the devil tempts him in three ways: 1) to be given all the kingdoms of the world, 2) to turn stones into bread, and 3) to throw himself off the temple expecting angels to catch him. While being subtle, all of the temptations would

23

cause Jesus to sin and forsake God. (For example, turning a stone into bread invalidates the fact that human beings need more than food.) Jesus responds negatively to all of the temptations by quoting the Old Testament. By doing so, Jesus refuses to embrace the social systems in place during this time. For instance, by not throwing himself off the temple expecting the angels to rescue him, he refutes the current oppressive religious system, members of whom would have seen the fall—and the angels' catch—and therefore would have proclaimed him as the Messiah (Kraybill 1978: 58, 65, 91).

We find many of the previous elements of wilderness experiences in Jesus' wilderness/ desert experience. For example, the Spirit leads Jesus into the desert. God's hand guides one into desert experiences. The themes of testing and choice are present as well. Jesus remains alone in the desert left to his own thoughts, musings, and temptations to turn away from God. Jesus has a choice to make decisions for or against God. Nothing implies the Father stands by to encourage him to remain faithful to his calling. We also know from this passage that temptations often appear good. During wilderness/desert times, many paths leading away from the road one has been called to travel will appear appealing—especially paths that lead on out of pain. These ways out, however, may not be what God wants and in fact, they may even have been initiated by the devil.

After Jesus' wilderness experience, we find him returning to Galilee full of the Spirit and ready to do ministry. This point signals the beginning of Jesus' ministry. His desert time served as preparation for ministry.

Key Points from Jesus' Isolation Experience

- God is sovereign in all isolation experiences.
- The enemy will always make attractive offers for leaders who are in isolation. There will always be temptations to take an easier way while in isolation or to get out of isolation altogether. Do not give into this temptation.

Case K. Paul, Time Alone for God's Formation

In Acts 9 we find the story of Saul's conversion as he travels to Damascus with orders in hand to persecute the Christians (After his conversion, Saul's name becomes Paul). As the Lord Jesus Christ confronts Saul, he blinds him and then asks why Saul persecutes him. Saul instantly knows who speaks to him and even calls Jesus "Lord." Saul remains blind for three days until Ananias lays hands on him to heal his sight. In these three days, Saul has the opportunity to think through all that had been said about Jesus—particularly the fact of Jesus' resurrection. At the end of these days, we find that Saul experienced a radical paradigm shift in which all that he had previously believed in was called into question. These three days of darkness were an intensified wilderness experience for Saul; even as externally he experienced physical darkness, internally he questioned everything he had placed his hope in. At the end of this period, Saul completely embraced Jesus Christ and gave his life for preaching the good news that Jesus Christ is the Son of God. We know from later writings, however, that Paul was only experiencing his first wilderness time in the three days of blindness. Paul also spent an undetermined amount of time in the desert of Arabia as well.

Although the book of Acts does not mention Paul's desert experience, Paul himself refers to it in the book of Galatians. In Gal. 1: 17, Paul writes that after his conversion, he went immediately to Arabia. Scholars have varying opinions as to why Paul went to Arabia. Some think that he went to preach the gospel; others think that he went to be alone with God in order to develop a relationship with God and to theologically think through the paradigm shift he had just experienced (Bruce 1991: 81). Because of Paul's own description of his call and his time in Arabia, and because of the authority with which Paul preached on his return to Damascus, I believe Paul had an intense, reflecting isolation experience in Arabia.

First of all, Paul himself states that no man has dictated or taught him his new-found gospel (Gal. 1:11,12). Rather, he states, it has been revealed to him directly by Jesus Christ. In direct contrast to how Paul received his teaching in the school of Pharisees at the feet of Gamaliel, Paul has now received his teaching via relationship with Jesus Christ as they communed in the desert of Arabia. All that Paul had known before was stripped in the Light of Jesus Christ—in order to reflect on this, he isolated himself from any human influence.

Secondly, practically every Scripture Paul had known up until his conversion had to be recast in the light of the revelation of Christ. This process, it seems, would take longer than the three days of darkness Paul experienced after being blinded. The fact that Paul begins preaching with the full authority of Scripture leads me to believe he has already gone through the process of reframing his theology in the context of his knowledge of Christ, and therefore, he preaches powerfully with conviction. We find a well-established theology and relationship with Christ which I believe was formed and solidified in a desert experience in Arabia.

Key Points from Paul's First Isolation Experience[14]

- Isolation experiences solidify paradigm shifts.
- Intense theological reflection can occur during isolation.
- Intimacy with Jesus empowers an isolation experience. This is ultimately the goal of any isolation time

Summary

A similar process or pattern can be detected in all the seasons of isolation found above (with the possible exception of Jesus' desert experience). This pattern has to do with a trans-

---

[14] Of interest to those who want more on isolation processing is Paul's other isolation experiences including one of the most important ones—his imprisonment. Out of these times comes some of our most important epistles.

formation in the identity of an individual before and after the isolation—for each, a process of stripping one's identity and restoring a new identity occurs. Joseph's isolation experience strips him of his favored son status in a favored family as he becomes a slave and a prisoner. God restores Joseph and makes him a world renowned leader. Moses' desert period strips him of his position of royalty and consequently, he becomes a shepherd in a foreign land. God calls Moses out of this foreign land to return and be his choice for the leader of the Hebrews. Elijah, once a mighty prophet, becomes the servant of a widow and her son. God expands his ministry, however, in the encounter with the Baal prophets. While Jesus' wilderness experience does not strip his identity, the people's perceptions of the Messiah are stripped. Jesus will not come into power using force, he will not be a welfare King, and he will not validate the oppressive religious system of the time (Kraybill 1978: 58). He will offer the Kingdom of God to those who believe as well as a spirituality not bound by a fastidious religious system, and he will offer more than mere bread—he will offer himself for eternal life. Isolation strips Paul of his identity as the "Pharisee of Pharisees" and in his restored identity, he becomes a powerful apostle to the gentiles. Thus, we see a pattern of stripping and restoring or recreating of identity during these desert times. And the most encouraging thing, God always involves himself in the process.

Two Types Of Isolation
Voluntary or Involuntary

Most of us don't like surprises, especially if they bring on painful shaping activities. Consider the case of Samuel Brengle.

Case L. Samuel Brengle—The Brick, Isolation and Ultimate Contribution

As Samuel walked out of the meeting hall, he reflected on the evening's events. It had not been a smooth meeting by any means with the disruption of the drunkard and Samuel's subsequent choice to have the man removed. Now, as Samuel was opening the door, he wondered where the man was and if he really should have thrown him out. Just as he stepped into the alley, Samuel was struck by something hard and weighty and dropped to the ground unconscious. As it turned out, the drunk man had been waiting for Samuel in the alley to shower him with his anger in the object of a brick. For the next six months, Samuel Logan Brengle fought for his life as a result of the injuries he received from the blow of the brick. Eventually Brengle recovered, but he was bedridden for two years. This was his isolation experience. It is interesting to note that Brengle actually thanked God for this period of time, for it was during this time that the Lord gave him profound insight into scripture and ministry. In fact, it was out of this time period that Brengle developed his creed and book *"Hints to Holiness"* which virtually revolutionized his evangelistic and renewal ministry. Because of this isolation period, hundreds if not thousands were saved in the years of crusades that followed. In later, years Brengle when thanking God for this time used to say, "No brick. No book!"[15]

As one can deduce from the above scenarios (Biblical and the Brengle scenario), there are many types of isolation and many ways one can enter an isolation period. For the most part, however, isolation experiences are distinctively either voluntary or involuntary. Brengle's was definitely involuntary. And it is these surprises—the involuntary kinds— that shake us.

Involuntary

Throughout our study of leaders' lives (including leaders in the Bible, Christian leaders in history and contemporary Christian leaders), we have found several types of involuntary isolation experiences. In these cases, the leader does not choose to take time away from ministry but is forced out of ministry as exemplified in the following reasons.

Involuntary Isolation Experiences—Defined

Definition   Involuntary Isolation refers to isolation experiences which are basically unexpected, which happen to a leader not by his/her choice, which the leader usually has little or no control over and which usually involve negative shaping activities.

---

[15]This simple statement holds much truth. For all of us who go through isolation can affirm the notion— without ... then no .... But it sometimes remains for us to reflect with a life long perspective to see this wonderful contrast.

- Sickness or injury—leaders cannot minister because they are bedridden.
- Imprisonment—leaders cannot minister because they are incarcerated.
- Organizational discipline—leaders cannot minister because they are being disciplined.
- War or natural disasters—leaders are set aside for periods of time due to events which they cannot control. And they cannot minister.

1) Isolation due to sickness or an accident—here leaders are set aside from ministry because of sickness or some type of injury (e.g. Samuel Logan Brengle). While I do not know of many theologians who would say that God inflicts upon his children sickness in order to teach them a lesson, God certainly uses these times to strengthen the faith of the leader. Like all isolation experiences, isolation due to sickness deepens one's relationship with God, and sickness may bring lessons regarding supernatural healing and prayer.

2) Isolation due to imprisonment—leaders are set aside from ministry because they are imprisoned. This type of isolation experience may not be common in our Western context; however, many brothers and sisters in more politically charged parts of the world have spent numerous months, if not years, in prison. Here the lessons of isolation relate to a deepening in one's mental capabilities and an intensified sense of urgency to accomplish the work of the gospel. The leader's faith is once again deepened as he/she holds on to Christ in the face of opposition or counter measures that would try to push for apostasy.

3) Personality Conflicts/Organizational Discipline—leaders are set aside because they are not functioning well

in their ministry or because they have had a conflict
with a supervisor and they are disciplined by not being allowed to participate in their normal ministry.
Leaders may also experience organizational discipline
if they have fallen into some type of sin and need to
take a break from ministry in order to work on their
problems. While the other involuntary isolation periods also lead to extreme brokenness, persons removed
from ministry because of organizational discipline
experience extreme brokenness if they will embrace
the time for what it is—a deepening, transformational
experience. As just mentioned, leaders in this isolation time learn the lessons incorporated into brokenness such as submission, not having one's identity be
engulfed in ministry and transformation of character.
It should be noted that leaders being disciplined or
removed may even be in the right and therefore un-
dergoing discipline unfairly. However, even if this is
the case, the lessons they will learn from this type of
isolation will be the same. We now turn to voluntary
types of isolation experiences.

Voluntary—Defined

Definition   Voluntary Isolation refers to isolation experi-
                   ences which are basically expected, which hap-
                   pen to a leader by his/her choice, which the
                   leader usually has some control over and which
                   usually involve expected shaping activities.

"I am finally getting the mentoring and perspective I have
needed." "I have never experienced renewal like this before."
"I did not realize reflecting on my life would be such hard
work. I feel like I am in intense therapy each week." "My
heart is filled with pain. I am finding it difficult to imagine
making it through each day."

As I have interacted with numerous leaders in voluntary
isolation, I have heard statements similar to these which con-

vey both the positive and the more difficult aspects of an isolation experience that is voluntary. In our observations of leaders' lives, we have categorized three types of voluntary isolation experiences.

Voluntary Isolation—Causes for Choosing [16]

Why do leaders choose to take time off from ministry? Here are some major reasons we have discovered.

- Self-choice for renewal
- Self-choice for education or training
- Self-choice for social base purposes

1)   **Self-choice for renewal**—here leaders choose to take a break from ministry in order to seek renewal. Our studies indicate that leaders need 3-4 renewal times over a life time. Selected isolation for renewal allows leaders to take a step back from ministry in order to reflect and seek God's direction for the next phase of ministry or life. The primary purpose for this time is to seek God's face and interact with the Lord. For this purpose leaders may choose to go to a monastery for a few weeks or go to a different city or an isolated cabin, so they are able to be fully out of their ministry context. They may to choose to pursue spiritual direction or sit under someone's guidance for a period of time in order to have a "spiritual check up."

2)   **Self choice for education or training**—leaders step out of ministry for a period of time in order to receive further equipping. Equipping for ministry can take place in a variety of contexts whether it be at a seminary, an institute, university, a conference, or a prolonged apprenticeship or internship. Leaders receiv-

[16] Clinton has proposed an interesting thesis regarding voluntary and involuntary isolation experiences. He suggests that regular choices of voluntary isolation experiences will lessen the need for involuntary isolation experiences.

ing the education or training usually gain a wider perspective on ministry as well as fresh ideas and vision for the future. Educational contexts also allow leaders to reflect on previous ministry resulting in a greater awareness of who they are as a minister. Both renewal and educational isolation experiences normally incorporate mentoring and guidance leading to a renewed sense of destiny. [17]

3) **Self-choice for social base**[18] Leaders may step out of full-time ministry due to the needs of family. One spouse may choose to take a break from a current ministry in order to invest in child rearing. Or a couple who has functioned with one of the partners in full-time ministry and the other in some type of secular job may choose to change roles for a period of time. Whatever the form it takes, this type of isolation results in a deepened relationship with God as individuals use the ordinariness of the day to practice the presence of God. Where previously in the context of ministry there might have been scheduled focused time to meet with God, it can be difficult to have a normal quiet time while being the primary care giver of the family. As they feed the children, clean the house or do the laundry they find Jesus in the ordinary routine of the day.

---

[17] This is a healthy thing—taking time of for study, that is, deliberately choosing isolation from ministry. For one of the major leadership lessons we have identified is, "Effective leaders maintain a learning posture all their lives." What is surprising sometimes is that isolation, in its emotional aspect, can affect a person deeply even in a chosen interlude primarily for educational purposes. My own opening illustration depicts this.

[18] Social base refers to the physical, emotional, and spiritual environment leaders minister from. It is the group of people who act as a support

The Fourfold Process A Leader Undergoes While In Isolation

Leaders undergo an observable process as they enter isolation. While different leaders may experience different nuances of the process, the overall process and the feelings that go along with the various stages of the process are fairly consistent and usually in the order given, though order may vary and certainly overlapping may occur. The four processes are usually more intensive in involuntary isolation experiences than in voluntary isolation experiences.

1. Stripping

Each summer as a child I used to visit my grandparents on the family ranch in Montana and as a teenager eventually worked for my grandparents for five summers. One summer my grandfather and I were cleaning out the barn and happened upon an old, broken chair.

My grandfather decided we would refurbish the chair, which I thought meant we would fix the chair and paint it to be used in the bunkhouse. A few minutes later, however, my grandfather brought out some turpentine and other chemicals along with some rags. He proceeded to show me how to remove the paint with the rags and turpentine. As I scrubbed the chair with the chemicals, I came upon layer after layer of different colored paint—white, yellow, green—all presumably matching a different era of the chair's life and service in a room. I finally reached what I thought to be the wood, but as it happened it was only a coat of varnish. Much to my disappointment this too had to come off. I thought I was finally going to get to paint! But my grandfather brought out the sand paper. I sanded and sanded and then sanded some more until finally I had reached the real wood of the chair—a beautiful oak. I was thrilled! My grandfather and I fixed the chair and put on a coat of stain which accented the beauty of the wood. I as the apprentice had learned the art of stripping and refinishing and only later did I discover that the Lord does this same type of process with us as we are in isolation.

I have watched many leaders enter periods of isolation for various reasons: a stripping process usually initiates the isolation. While leaders can be stripped of many things while in a period of isolation (money, family, health, etc.) they are primarily stripped of their ministry identity. "In my home country I pastored a church of 1000 people and led many people to the Lord each week. Here in the U.S. I am nobody. I feel like a child." "I have started several missions organizations. People have looked to me for leadership for all of my life. Now I am not leading anyone or anything." "I used to teach young leaders who were going to be pastors. Now all I can do is get out of bed each morning and sit in my rocking chair hoping to make it through another day of pain." "No one knows me here. I do not have a history with anyone in this place. I feel lonely and misunderstood."

During a season of isolation, leaders are no longer the pastor of the church, the president of an organization, or the campus minister. The Lord removes the various identities that ministry places upon a leader and strips the leader down to the core of who he/she has been created to be (the identity that the Lord places in him/her). This can be a very daunting process for often who we are in any given situation is defined by what the external cues tell us to be. Any context or ministry has a particular culture which defines who the leader should be. As the Lord strips the external identities (sometimes a leader adopts various identities for different situations), leaders often experience the pain of being stripped and the confusion of not knowing who they really are. They have adapted to many situations and organizational cultures and have often forsaken their own identity in order to succeed. After the ministry identity is removed, feelings of insecurity depression and emotional pain may follow. Leaders in this state question who they are and long to have the external identity again.

Leaders who have been removed from leadership because of organizational discipline—whether deserved or not—experience a great deal of rejection in the stripping process. One missionary had been perceived as a threat to the insecure leader of her team for years because she was a gifted and competent leader. After several years of feeling threatened the mission leader sent the missionary home accusing her of politicizing with the purpose or taking over leadership of the team. Of course the missionary was crushed and left the field thinking that all of her dreams of having an impact for God's Kingdom were hopelessly lost. She arrived back in the States hurt angry and rejected wondering if she would ever be able to do ministry again. Her calling to the country where she had poured out her life for five years seemed like a cruel joke— in her pain she wondered where God was.

The pain of the stripping process can be severe as God's sand paper removes the external identities. Even if leaders have entered a season of isolation by their own choice, the stripping process remains painful. In this process leaders discover how much they rely on the affirmation of ministry. Leaders discover how addicted they are to the success of ministry. They may even discover that they are getting their needs met by helping others resolve pain. As the Lord leaves leaders empty handed without a ministry to tell them who they are, they experience a deep sense of loss and emotional pain. They begin to ask questions about who they are and about where their value lies "Is it enough to just have my relationship with God? What if I never do ministry again?" The stripping process has uncovered the leader's deep need for God.

Feelings One May Experience in Stripping

- emotional pain
- hurt
- confusion
- distrust
- joy
- depression
- rejection
- insecurity
- embarrassment
- not belonging
- fear
- relief
- anger
- sadness

2. Wrestling with God

At this point the person has entered what some may call "the dark night of the soul."[19] Leaders in this state hunger for God and search for their true identity.

As I asked the following question of the missionary sitting in my office, his face immediately turned downward. He was nearing the end of his stripping process and in the midst of the excruciating soul searching one undergoes during this period. "If you could not return to your leadership position in Kenya who would you be?" His reply revealed the perplexity of experiencing isolation. "I do not know who I would be out of this ministry." Much of his self-worth depended on his ministry role and accomplishments.

---

[19] This is a term flowing from St. John of the Cross. It is essentially a time in which God seemingly can't be found. And in St. John's stages of spirituality it is a boundary time which precedes entrance into a sublime experience of union with God. But more popularly it is used today to speak of a hard time a leader goes through in which there is confusion, emotional distress, and a lack of the sensed presence of God.

It may not be readily apparent, but God uncovers one's core identity in the stripping process. For leaders who are willing to go through this process, an honest wrestling with God occurs next. They ask many deep searching questions of God such as, "Who have you created me to be?" "What is my true identity—apart from outside ministry?" Perhaps leaders even discover during this time that they have been doing ministry under the false pretext of serving—they have been doing ministry in an addictive pattern of getting their needs met by helping to resolve someone else's pain and at the same time not addressing their own pain or character.

Having come to the point of feeling left to deal with one's self, the leader turns to God for the answers to his/her identity questions. The desperation to embrace one's identity fuels the fire of seeking and honest questioning of God. Rather than being defined by the praise of others and the success of ministry, the person begins to look to God for true definition. In the midst of wrestling, it becomes very apparent that the minister cannot return to ministry unless these issues are resolved. The biblical narrative which involves Jacob returning to the land of promise brings particular insight to this phase of isolation.

After escaping from Laban (Gen. 32), Jacob sets out to return to the land that has been promised to him by the blessing of his father Isaac. Yet Jacob realizes his crisis of identity as he nears the land of Palestine—he knows that the blessing he did receive from his father he received by deception and therefore, he fears that he does not truly have God's blessing. His identity is one of deception rather than the one chosen as the intended recipient of the favored blessing of God for land, descendants, and being a blessing to all nations. To compound matters further Jacob knows that Esau his brother is on the way out to meet him—presumably to kill him since Jacob robbed Esau of their father's blessing. So as a result of an isolation experience Jacob knows his true identity as a deceiver and in a climatic moment of his isolation time—the night before he meets Esau—Jacob tenaciously demands God to transform his identity.

The night before Jacob meets his brother Esau, he wrestles with the angel of the Lord (presumably a theophany) all night. Jacob will not let the Lord go until he has blessed him—until he affirms his true identity. The Lord gives Jacob this affirmation and blessing and at the same time calls forth his true identity by changing his name from Jacob ("deceiver") to Israel ("one who struggles with God"). Jacob unrelentingly holds on to God until the Lord calls forth and reveals who he has been created to be.

Likewise persons in isolation must tenaciously hold on to God and embrace their true identity as the Lord calls it forth. The leader in this stage realizes that nothing will satisfy and bring life but God. This in turn increases and facilitates a greater depth of intimacy with God.

Feelings One May Experience in Wrestling

- confusion
- lack of confidence
- Who am I?
- more emotional pain
- questioning
- spiritual hunger

3. Increased Intimacy

I HAVE GOT TO HAVE MORE OF YOU LORD AND I HAVE GOT TO HAVE IT NOW! This oft repeated cry during my own times of isolation characterizes my hunger for God and desire to hear his creating voice in my life. During the wrestling phase, a desperate intensity enters one's relationship with God. Having realized that one is not what one's ministry is and having wrestled with God begging him to call forth one's created identity, one realizes that life holds no value apart from an honest, intimate relationship with the Lord.

This stage of isolation encompasses a number of different characteristics, among them openness, honesty, weakness, or brokenness and vulnerability. Many leaders do not stay in isolation long enough to experience this intimacy, for the feel-

ings that come with isolation become too intense. If they do
however make it to this stage of isolation, often they will not
embrace this stage of isolation because it goes against how
they perceive themselves as the strong leader who never has a
need or a problem.

Much of the evangelical Christian culture along with the
Protestant work ethic, pushes leaders to never admit their
weakness and their needs. However leaders in isolation become acutely aware of how much they need God and others
and this need drives them into intimacy. Embracing the fact
that one is "poor in spirit" (Mt. 5) is the first step in the
quest for intimacy. Being honest with God and with others
becomes a vital part of this process. Honesty with God means
that one expresses the feelings that seem so extreme, rather
than shoving them out of reach. Honesty with God means
that one expresses the questions in one's heart and holds on
tenaciously for the answer. Honesty with God means that one
expresses the character flaws one is discovering and asks him
to change them.

Leaders in isolation discover they are not as put together
and in control as they thought they were. Rather, they need a
physician. This critical realization leads to an important transformation in isolation, for in this stage of the process God
enters to meet the needs of leaders and also brings others to
create a sense of interdependency, which is crucial for when
the leaders eventually enter ministry again. Admitting one's
needs is almost always a humbling process, especially if one
comes from a background where it is not acceptable to be weak.
My family heritage comes from a stock of pioneering farmers
and ranchers. Rarely will anyone in my family ask for help or
admit when they have done something wrong. In fact if someone has a problem, it is usually assumed that he/she will figure it out on his/her own and it is not permissible to "burden" someone else. Therefore learning to admit my needs to
God and to others was a difficult part of increasing intimacy
in my life. The breakthrough came during an isolation time

in which I practically had no choice but to be honest about my feelings and needs, for I was dying an emotional death in my hidden world—the world of my heart. Interdependent communication and caring brought the life of the Lord I so desperately needed.

As intimacy with God and others increases, the importance of having a ministry on "the cutting edge" decreases. Leaders also realize that the external part of them that most people see is not the true part. They find freedom in allowing others to see their heart as leaders. During this time God affirms leaders for who he has created them to be, not for what they can accomplish in ministry. This severs the ties to having identity through successful ministry, and leaders realize satisfaction in being in the presence and loving arms of Jesus.

Feelings One May Experience in Intimacy

- yearning
- desperation
- brokenness
- freedom

- vulnerability
- glimpse of hope
- affirmation

4. Release to Look Toward the Future

One aside related to God leading a person out of isolation: one must wait until God leads him/her out of the wilderness for the temptation to leave before will always be present. When he was in the wilderness, Jesus ate nothing in his forty days of fasting and at the end of the time he was hungry. So the devil tempted him to make stones turn into bread—tempted him to eat. In isolation one is tempted to get satisfied, to get out of pain, out of isolation. Yet a premature departure from the desert may circumvent the refining/transforming process.

As the reader will find in every biblical example of a person in isolation, and as we have found in most every case study we have explored, God eventually brings leaders out of isolation. He is faithful. There comes an intuitive point in which leaders begin to look toward the future. God, by his Spirit, gently gives persons permission to begin looking outward again for a return to ministry and to begin exiting the isolation period. Sometimes the Lord radically pulls leaders out of isolation, for example, by instigating their release from prison, bringing them through a paradigm shift, or by healing their sickness. More often, however, God quietly releases leaders to begin the process of exploring the next stage of their lives by sending a divine contact[20] or an opportunity that matches their vision and the transformation that has occurred during the isolation period. Either way, the leader entering this phase will have a quiet peace when looking toward the future, rather than a restless desire to escape the pain of isolation.

Feelings One May Experience
When Looking Toward the Future

- patience
- hope
- frustration
- peace

- joy
- longing
- excitement

---

20 In Clinton's leadership emergence theory this is the technical name for the guidance process in which God brings along a person at a timely moment to intervene with a clarifying word, usually about the next steps in guidance.

Table 1—Summary of Fourfold Processes in Isolation

Process	Purpose	Attendant Feelings
1. Stripping	Usually a breaking process that prepares a person to want to go deep with God.	Emotional Pain, Hurt, Confusion, Distrust, Joy, Depression, Rejection, Insecurity, Embarrassment, Not belonging, Fear, Relief, Anger, Sadness
2. Wrestling with God	Turns the experience from a why to a what and creates a hunger for God.	Confusion, Lack of Confidence, Who am I?, More Emotional Pain, Questioning, Spiritual Hunger.
3. Increased Intimacy with God.	Forms a hunger for and a deepened relationship with God which will affect all future ministry since ministry flows out of being.	Yearning, Desperation, Brokeness, Freedom, Vulnerability, Glimpse of Hope, Affermation.
4. Looking forward to the future.	Frees up the person to know more of God, Experience more of God, and to expectantly look to God's continued presence in life and ministry.	Patience, Hope, Frustration, Peace, Joy, Longing, Excitement.

Case Study M: Watchman Nee

Watchman Nee's newly founded church was growing as ment and women responded to his heart penetrating evangelistic messages. Yet during these first few years, Nee barely had the strength to preach the messages and often had to rest for days after a trip or a speaking engagement—he had tuberculosis. Because of his illness, Nee experienced an isolation time early in his ministry. All of the above processes are evident in his isolation experience.

As Nee was isolated and struggling with his illness day after day, he began to question the Christian faith he had so readily embraced. The questioning led him to discover that he had embraced Christianity with a focus on externals—a smile always on his face, a look that had the appearance of victorious Christian living. Yet, now he feared he might be losing his faith. In reality, however, the Lord was stripping Nee of a simplistic view of Christianity which overlooked honest questioning and wrestling. He writes

> I thought a true Christian should smile from morning to night. If at any time he shed a tear he had ceased to be victorious. I thought too that a Christian must be unfailingly courageous. If under any circumstances he showed the slightest Sign of fear he had fallen short of my standard. (Kinnear 1973: 83)

The Lord eventually stripped Nee of this false external view of Christianity, but not before allowing him to experience the struggle and wrestling in his faith. Nee wrestled with his identity as a Christian and he wrestled with the expectations others had placed on his life. God had given him the identity of a child of God, yet there was still extreme pressure from his former teachers who thought he had thrown his life away by engaging in pastoral ministry.

The sickness continued and Nee begged/demanded—that the Lord heal him. He had a consuming call to ministry and he felt compelled to fulfill his calling. Yet, as is so often the case during a season of isolation, God was strangely silent until Nee finally gave up and embraced his isolation refusing to demand healing anymore. "Lord I trust You. I have dropped the matter of my healing here!" (Kinnear 1973:81)

The months dragged on and eventually Nee managed to maintain a quasi-isolation lifestyle. He preached when he could and then rested. The pattern continued in this vein for quite sometime until ultimately he had to rest for an extended period of time. It was during this time that Nee discovered profound insight into what it means to have a relationship with God and what it means to be a Christian.

When Nee came across Paul's words "as sorrowful" in 2 Corinthians, he was struck to the very core of his being.

A great Christian who shed "many tears" who could be "perplexed" and who could even "despair of" life itself must be very human. Is it possible he asked that Paul despaired? This was just where he himself had been! "I discovered", he says "that Paul was a man and the very sort of man I know." There began to dawn on him the secret of Christianity that is summarized in the words: "We have this treasure in earthen vessels to show that the transcendent power belongs to God and not to us." Now as he learned to trust God hourly for his very life he came to a new place of rest in Him. (Kinnear, 1973:83)

It was not long after this that Nee's health stabilized again and he was able to return to fulltime ministry. The isolation profoundly influenced his theology, his relationship with God and his identity as a Christian. He was truly transformed in many regards. From Nee's isolation experience we learn that:

3 Major Results in Needs Life Via Isolation Processing

God used isolation: • to transform identity.
                              • to introduce a paradigm shift.
                              • to deepen his relationship with the leader.

The following table summarizes the process of isolation and the evidence of this process in the lives of several of the leaders we have explored thus far. While the results of isolation differ for each leader, the process of isolation is similar.

Table 2
Isolation Examples and Their Experience of the
Fourfold Process

	Stripping	Wrestling	Intimacy	Future
Joseph	Identity as the favored son.	No apparent wrestling	Demonstration of a strong prayer life throughout.	Positioned through isolation for future ministry.
Moses	Identity as an Egyptain leader with the power to act.	Much wrestling when God called him back into ministry	Met with God "face-to-face".	Called into ministry from isolation.
Elijah	Unknown.	Unknown.	Deep dependence on God for daily sustenance.	Called into ministry from isolation.
Israelites	Identity as Egyptian slaves.	Much wrestling with their identity as slaves and God's calling to be his people.	Worship life established.	Prepared to enter the land as a united people who worship one God.
Jesus	No.	To not give into temptation.	Demonstrates trust in and intimacy with the Father.	Preparation for public ministry.
Paul	Identity as a Pharisee bound by the Law.	Theological reflection.	Develops a relationship with God for the first time.	Transition from Pharisaic ministry to the ministry of Jesus Christ.
Watchman Nee	External identity focus as a Christian.	Theological reflection and what he had given up to follow the Lord.	Embraces honesty and rest in the Lord.	Brings insights into ministry for proper theological contextualization.

THREE FRUITFUL RESULTS OF ISOLATION EXPERIENCES

It is crucial to note that God never leaves anyone in isolation indefinitely, and when one enters isolation, God's faithful character provides everything needed to endure the experience. When the appropriate time comes—perhaps when the person has been adequately refined in the crucible of the wilderness—God intervenes and calls the person out of the wilderness. In a matter of minutes God moved Joseph from prison to a leadership position second only to Pharaoh (Joseph hardly had time to shave and get cleaned up!). God moved Moses and Elijah from places of obscurity to establish them as the leader and prophet of the Israelites. After 40 years in the wilderness God led the Israelites into the promised land. When leaders move out of isolation they carry the fruit of isolation— transformation—in their being. Isolation produces three types of transformation: 1) inward transformation 2) spiritual transformation and 3) ministerial transformation.

1. Inward Transformation

Intense transformation occurs in the lives of those in isolation beginning with the process of breaking and stripping a former identity and the subsequent realization of created identity. Joseph, Moses, and Paul are prime examples of this process. All three had used their position or identity to lead in a way that seemed right to them but was completely opposite of God's purposes. All three were set aside for a period of time during which it seemed that their lives of ministry or position of leadership was over. All experienced an intense period of brokenness during which there were no indications that the period would ever end. Yet at the end of the period, all three emerged refined by God through the experience as humble, God-dependent leaders ready for their new calling. Joseph was no longer an arrogant immature boy taunting his family, but a wise man who had a single heart toward God and who knew God's faithfulness. Moses became a humble leader who spoke with God face-to-face. Paul's life purpose changed from being a man who followed the Law in every respect—and forced others to do so as well—to a man in love with Jesus and filled with passion to share the gospel. For all three the process of isolation must have been excruciating and frightening; yet the result was sweet and full of hope. Their relationship with God was secure for he was faithful to see them through their desert experiences.

Likewise leaders undergo transformation through the brokenness experienced in isolation. While painful, the resulting transformation brings the freedom of humility—the leader does not have to match up to some perceived external expectation. Again, brokenness points the way toward discovering who God has created the leader to be, which leads to another aspect of inward transformation—true identity.

Instead of finding identity in the ministry or in what one does, transformed leaders find identity by looking at the Artist, by looking toward the Author. Having experienced the stripping and wrestling that reveals who God has created them to be, broken leaders can now embrace their true identity wholeheartedly and enter ministry knowing their giftedness as well as their weakness. Thus, when the pressure comes to perform or be someone they are not, leaders can return to the roots of who God has created them to be.

Brokenness and discovery of true ide]
character barriers which have an impact c
leaders have been unable to have intim
fear anyone getting too close. Perhaps leaders ...
dicted to ministry because they ignore their own pain by deal-
ing with others' pain. Perhaps leaders have been addicted to
the praise of others and are using ministry as a platform for
praise. A period of isolation addresses all these character issues because one's true character and motivation is revealed
in the process. Since God strips to reveal or strips to bring
light to the internal situation, he also brings the healing needed
to move beyond these character barriers whether through
prayer, counseling and/or behavioral change.

Finally inner transformation produces vulnerable leaders
who honestly struggle. These vulnerable leaders do not hide
behind her weaknesses, but openly share them with God and
with others. These vulnerable leaders do not fear being viewed
as weak and incompetent, but openly ask for help and for
prayer. These leaders find freedom in vulnerability instead of
frantically trying to appear as if they have it all together.

Table 3
Inward Transformation— Before and After Isolation

Before	After
• performance orientation	• freedom in humility
• arrogance/pride	• humble learner
• double minded/serving humans	• faithful/serving God
• defined by external queues	• defined by God
• addictive behaviors	• freedom
• power hungry	• a servant leader
• hidden/controlling	• a vulnerable leader

Spiritual Transformation

We see God's provision for those in isolation in all of the scenarios mentioned earlier. The Scripture states over and over again that God was with Joseph (Gen. 39: 2 3 21 23), and in the wanderings of the Israelites the LORD provided their food and made it so their clothes would not wear out. God's faithfulness can be seen in the life of Elijah as the Lord sends ravens to feed him and miraculously multiplies the widow's flour and oil for three years. God demonstrates his faithfulness by providing for those in isolation and by eventually leading them out of isolation. In doing so he shapes and forms faith in those who have experienced an isolation period. This in turn increases the leader's dependence on God as well as the leader's ability to listen and hear God's voice. The spirit of the leader moves with God's spirit.

People coming out of isolation experience a renewed spirituality. Since they have gone to the bottom of the pit and discovered bare bones faith and faithfulness, they find a renewed confidence that Christianity is truth. They also know that their faith and God's faithfulness to them do not depend on any circumstance.

Most importantly these transformed leaders have a deeper more intimate relationship with God which is primary for their lives. Just as one enjoys the company of a friend who knows him/her deeply, these leaders enjoy God. An honesty has entered their relationship with God which will not be stolen by the "shoulds" and the "ought to" of a religious system. Just as Jesus received love and friendship from the Father, so too increased intimacy in the lives of leaders will allow them to go forth in the confidence of the Father's love listening for his voice, moving when he moves, speaking when he speaks (Jn. 5:19-20). These leaders will engage in life and ministry with true spiritual authority rather than positional authority or manipulation.

Table 4
Spiritual Transformation— Before and After I|

Before	After
• self-seeking confidence	• dependence on G(
• spiritual dullness	• spiritual acuteness
• superficial prayer life	• deep intimacy
• one way conversation with God	• hear and how God's voice
• untested faith	• faithful maturity

3. Ministerial Transformation

The character formation of leaders who experience isolation has a direct impact on their ministry. Transformation via isolation results in leaders who listen to the voice of God and trust God's leading. Their relationship with God has been deepened. These leaders know God's provision and God calls forth their created identity for service in ministry and mission. In actuality they become more who they truly have been created to be. These transformed leaders do not carry their own agenda into ministry but rather the Lord's agenda. As a result of isolation, God transforms leaders' motives for ministry and moves them back into ministry with new-found freedom.

The leader's discovery of the Source and Sustainer of ministry is a critical transformation born out of isolation. Ministry training and experience often point to different tactics that produce successful and fruitful ministry for example, church growth analysis, preaching styles, outreach strategies, healing ministry, etc. The temptation always comes for the leader to rely on the latest technique or method in order to have a successful ministry. Those who have been through isolation discover, however, that one cannot do ministry by only relying on a technique or fad. In fact, in the light of an experience of isolation, all methods and techniques seem empty and made of straw. The leader has turned instead to the true Source and Sustainer of ministry—Jesus Christ—trusting in his creativ-

ful ministry.

...sformation often expands the
...nd may position him/her for a
... the Pharaoh recognized the
...omoted Joseph from a prison
... In doing so, God through
...ed food for Egypt and the surround-
...ing the famine. Elijah had experienced the
...ness of God and thus was eager to partner with God
in the power encounter with the Baal prophets. As a result,
all the neighboring nations witnessed the sovereignty and
power of the God of Israel. Paul's conversion and calling, which
resulted from isolation, directly focused on the Gentiles—on
all nations- being incorporated into the family of God. As we
can see then, God's purposes in processing a leader through
an isolation period may be to expand the leader's ministry
influence because of the character formation that occurs or
may be to position a leader in the appropriate place for future
ministry.

Table 5
Ministerial Transformation
Before and After Isolation

Before	After
• happen to do ministry	• follow God's leading in ministry
• unaware of gifts	• make ministry decisions based on gifting
• happen upon a ministry role	• make proactive choices for the appropriate ministry role
• do ministry to meet own needs	• ministering with God as the source
• minister in own strength	• minister by relying on God's strength
• do faddish ministry	• do purposeful ministry
• small sphere of influence	• usually a larger sphere of influence.

PSALM 42—SIX THINGS TO HEIGHTEN DEVELOPMENT IN ISOLATION

One of my favorite Psalms depicts a person who is experiencing isolation.

As a deer longs for flowing streams, so my soul longs for you, O God, My soul thirsts for God, for the living God. When shall I come and behold the face of God? My tears have been my food day and night, while people say to me continually "Where is your God"?"

These things I remember, as I pour out my soul: how I went with the throng, and led them in procession to the house of God, with glad shouts and songs of thanksgiving, a multitude keeping festival. Why are you cast down, O my soul, and why are you disquieted within me? Hope in God; for I shall again praise him, my help and my God.

My soul is cast down within me; therefore I remember you from the land of Jordan and of Hermon, from Mount Mizar. Deep calls to deep at the thunder of your cataracts; all your waves and your billows have gone over me. By day the LORD commands his, steadfast love, and at night his song is with me, a prayer to the God of my life.

I say to God, my rock, "Why have you forgotten me? Why must I walk about mournfully because the enemy oppresses me?" As with a deadly wound in my body, my adversaries taunt me, while they say to me continually, "Where is your God?"

Why are you cast down, O my soul, and why are you disquieted within me ? Hope in God; for I shall again praise him, my help and my God. (Psalm 42 NRSV)

Who Will Experience Isolation?—You Will Most Likely!

In our study of leaders in the Bible, leaders in history, and contemporary leaders, we have found that approximately 95 % of all leaders go through periods of isolation.[21] YOU WILL EXPERIENCE ISOLATION! And while a season of isolation may feel like a white water raft trip down a river of emotion and inner processing, you can be proactive in order to embrace what God has for you during isolation. You can determine beforehand to go deep with God knowing his purposes during isolation. In the following section, you will find ways in which you can embrace all that God has for you during a season of isolation and continue your leadership development during isolation. I am exegeting Psalm 42 as a spring board for thoughts that will help you develop while in isolation.

---

[21]We have amassed over 1000 case studies of leaders in the School of World Mission leadership concentration. About 95 % of these have one or more isolation experiences as shaping factors in their lives.

1. Be Honest

"When shall I come and behold the face of God? . . . Why have you forgotten men? Why must I walk about mournfully because the enemy oppresses me?" We do not know the circumstance or occasion in which the psalmist wrote this cry (Perowne 1966, 347). Some suggest that David wrote it when he was facing Absalom and was under God's judgment for killing Uriah (II Sam. 17). We do know that the psalmist has been a leader of God and has even led many "in procession to the house of God" (v. 4b). We also know that this leader finds himself far away from the temple and from the people he used to lead (v. 6b). The questions the psalmist asks of God illumine the first critical response of one who is in isolation—be honest.

Learning to be honest is one of the major lessons for any leader in isolation. Taking the example of the psalmist as our model, honesty means bringing the burning questions of your heart to God. Honesty even means expressing your anger at God for putting you in isolation. Honesty means wrestling and struggling with God during the isolation. We also see that the psalmist honestly shares the feelings he experiences during his isolation with God—"my soul longs for you O God.... my tears have been my food day and night... . I pour out my soul.... Why are you cast down O my soul and why are you disquieted within me? . . . all your waves and billows have gone over me." One of God's greatest gifts to you during isolation will be the uncovering of feelings in your heart. Because these are your feelings and God has created you as a feeling being, express them back to God and share them with those who are close to you.

Many Christians find it difficult to share their feelings because feelings, especially if they are anger or sadness, tend to be viewed negatively. Yet, if God created us with feelings, then as a loving Father he validates our feelings—all of them. What we do or do not do with our feelings is the critical decision. Since isolation reveals and illicits many feelings, sharing those feelings appropriately is paramount. I find many, however, who find it very difficult to share feelings of any kind. For these leaders I recommend that they read through the Psalms everyday; it is most effective when they are read out loud. The Psalms contain every feeling known to humans, and the psalmists express all of their feelings to God in prayer. Thus a steady discipline of reading the Psalms helps one get in touch with his/her feelings and in turn enables one to express those feelings.

Five Steps Toward Honesty

1. Get in touch with your feelings.
2. Express your feelings either in your journal or to a friend and/or spouse.
3. Ask God the questions which are burning in your heart, the questions you wrestle with during your season of isolation.
4. Read the Psalms out loud everyday for ten minutes. After each sitting, journal any response you have to the Psalms or to God.
5. Tell a friend your struggles and your fears.

2. Remember

"These things I remember.... therefore I remember you from the land of Jordan and of Hermon." The psalmist remembers his past ministry and he remembers God. Since seasons of isolation often ensue prior to a change of ministry or a major transition in one's life, reflection becomes an important part of the process of isolation as well. By reflection, I am not simply referring to remembering the glory days of ministry, wishing that you could return. Rather God has developed in you important values, attitudes, skills, and experiences from your previous time in ministry. You carry all of these, though unseen, with you into the next phase of your life of ministry; therefore it is crucial to articulate what these values and experiences are before moving on to the next phase of ministry. Articulation brings to the forefront intuitive suppositions which drive your ministry. As you think back over the last years of your ministry life, what are the highlights of your time in ministry? When did you enjoy ministry the most? When did you experience the most freedom in ministry? What is your attitude toward conflict? Are there periods of conflict that still puzzle you? How can you resolve conflict the next time? What did you find painful in your life of ministry?

Another important aspect of remembering has to do with your own leadership emergence. Who is God creating you to be as a leader? Use the period of isolation to reflect on your gifting—natural abilities, acquired skills and spiritual gifts. How have you experienced your gifting? Whose leadership style are you attracted to?[22] Go back over your experiences as a leader and think through what type of leader you are. For instance, are you more relational or task oriented? Do you enjoy being a visionary and moving others toward God's purposes in their lives? Do you prefer behind the scenes organization? Everyone's leadership style will vary, but you can notice the broad strokes of who you are as a leader.

Finally, remember who God is. As you read the Bible, notice the many promises God gives to his people and notice his faithfulness to keep these promises. A promise to Abraham in Genesis 12 was fulfilled in every generation following and finally fulfilled in us through our relationship with Jesus. Notice also how God views you as his beloved child. Notice your inheritance. All these truths bring comfort to your period of isolation especially since it often seems that God is very distant. Go deep into the truth of God's Word and the truth of his faithfulness will be formed in you. This type of remembering leads to the next part of developing in isolation— have hope/keep perspective.

---

[22] The "like attracts like" principle often gives insight into one's leadership giftedness. If you are attracted to someone's leadership, it is likely that you have or will have similar gifting.

Seven Helpful Exercises Toward Remembering

1. Write a brief history of your previous ministry.
2. Take time to thank God for your previous ministry experience and remember nothing happened by accident but can be used by God to shape you.
3. From your history, highlight at least five key values that you gained during your time of ministry and that inform your future ministry. What are these values and why are they important?
4. Write what you perceive as your gifting including your natural abilities, acquired skills and spiritual gifts.
5. Remember and write about a time you enjoyed ministry and felt fulfilled doing ministry.
6. Write about any unresolved conflict that still influences you.
7. Immerse yourself in the Scriptures and notice God's promises.

3. Have Hope—Keep Perspective

"Hope in God; for I shall again praise him my help and my God." Just as the deadness of winter eventually gives way to the life of spring, so too dying during isolation comes to an end and you experience the life of resurrection. As I have stated before, ISOLATION WILL END, and God is always faithful to bring the leader out of isolation. You can expect to have seasons of isolation and you can expect to come out of seasons of isolation. Knowing that the pain of isolation will not last indefinitely gives you hope in the midst of it. I can guarantee that even though the pain of isolation is very difficult, you will like the results of a season of isolation in your life. You will like the freedom, you will like knowing who God has created you to be, and you will like the depth of relationship you will experience with the Lord.

In the above sections I have tried to outline the stages of isolation. Allow these stages to give you perspective and insight as to where you find yourself in the process of isolation.

If you are being stripped, await the depth of intimacy that comes as you discover who you are. If you are wrestling with God, await the bright future that God will bring as you develop an honest relationship with him. In other words, know the purposes of seasons of isolation and endeavor to discern what God is working into your life. Having these in mind will help you keep perspective even during the more difficult days and weeks.

Five Helpful Suggestions Toward Having Hope

1. Understand the process of isolation and remember it does end.
2. Reflect on the promises God has given you and has fulfilled in your journey with him. He will be faithful to fulfill these promises.
3. Return to the history you have written earlier and notice any inklings of destiny. Notice situations or incidents that somehow indicate what your ministry destiny is.
4. With some of your destiny experiences in mind, reflect on what God may be trying to form in you during this isolation time to prepare you for your future.
5. Keep a log of experiences of divine affirmation and ministry affirmation and periodically read this log to remind yourself of God's working in your life.

4. Get a Mentor

Having a mentor who has been through isolation will provide you with a spiritual guide to help give perspective and will provide a friend to empathize with the darkness that one experiences during isolation. There will be many times while you are in isolation that you will need to hear that things will be okay, that you will come out of this time, and that you will like God's transformation in your life. Mentors can also help you be honest about your experience of isolation and ask the deeper questions which reveal your heart. Finally, a discerning mentor can help you see the barriers you have in your heart toward honesty and intimacy. A discerning mentor can play a crucial role in the character formation God brings during isolation by telling you the truth about who you are and encouraging you to go deeper.

Five Suggestions About Mentoring

1. Interview several potential mentors who have gone through an isolation or wilderness time to see who your heart connects with.
2. Ask the mentor to meet with you and hold you accountable while you are in this isolation time.
3. Agree upon a format for your meetings and on how often you will meet.
4. Share with your mentor the things you feel God may be wanting to transform during this isolation time.
5. With your mentor's counsel establish goals for your mentoring relationship that facilitate what God is doing in your life during the isolation time.

5. Listen for the Voice of God

During the darkest moments of one of my seasons of isolation, I feared that God had left me—that I would forever be placed on the shelf to watch others engage in fruitful ministry while I sat on the bench. Working at the fudge store my days were filled with seemingly mundane things—washing windows, sweeping the floor, mopping the floor, making bows, and cooking fudge. I found it difficult to find any spiritual meaning in my daily activities. God seemed silent. In these moments I could often hear the voice of the enemy placing doubts in my heart; "You see, God has abandoned you—that's just like Him. When you need Him the most He is not around to reassure. You will never experience joy again," and so on. To combat these lies which were vying for my attention and to listen for God's voice, I tried several spiritual disciplines to remind me of the truth of God's presence and the truth of God's commitment to me.

The first discipline is called "practicing the presence of God" (Lawrence 1958). In this discipline the goal is to be aware of God's presence in every moment. I began by thinking about God every hour on the hour. As the hour approached I turned the thoughts of my heart toward God, asking if he had anything to say to me and waiting to hear his response to my heart. I also took those moments to prayerfully tell him what I was thinking about or feeling. As the discipline of checking in with Jesus was established each hour, I tried to shorten the intervals between checking in until finally I could consistently remember his presence in each of my daily activities. Sometimes God's voice would speak quietly to my heart about the customer I was waiting on by giving me a word of encouragement for that person. Sometimes God's voice encouraged me. Many times I still found him silent and would then need to work through my feelings about his seeming silence.

Much of the struggle during my isolation time was with the lies of the enemy either about God or about me. For these times I chose a particular meditation of truth to repeat out loud in my prayer time and repeat silently in my mind during the day. For instance, from the Psalm at the beginning of the chapter I would choose "Hope in God; for I shall again praise him, my help and my God," and I would repeat this verse for a week as I practiced the presence of God. Sometimes I chose more of a liturgical meditation such as, "Lord Jesus Christ Son of God grant me your peace," and this would be my prayer throughout the day. Other times I chose a meditation that implanted a truth about who I am as God's daughter such as "I am a daughter of the Most High God. He creates and calls forth my being." Meditations such as the above ushered truth into my life which kept me grounded when the waves of depression hit. They also acted to keep me aware of God's presence that I might hear the whisper of his voice. Perhaps one of these disciplines will work for you as well.

Three Helps Toward Hearing God's Voice

1. Get a copy of Brother Lawrence's "The Practice of the Presence of God" and try this method of being constantly aware of God's presence.
2. Meditate on truth that is appropriate to your situation and to what you struggle with.
3. Try the discipline of "centering prayer." Choose a verse in Scripture to meditate on. Read the verse out loud several times and allow the Lord to highlight one of the words in the verse. Focus on this word for ten minutes. (I find that it is best to set an alarm; otherwise I am too distracted by worrying about how long I have been praying.)

6. Embrace Isolation

During the darker moments of isolation, you will be tempted to get out of isolation either by filling your schedule with activity or accepting ministry opportunities too soon. Especially if you are motivated by praise or get your needs met by serving others, it will be especially tempting to avoid the reality of isolation by opting out of it. Apart from isolation experiences that are involuntary, you will always have the choice of getting out of isolation. However, an early exit from isolation circumvents the transformation God brings during isolation. As you enter isolation determine to embrace all that God has for you while in isolation. Determine to go with him deep into your heart, determine to ask the deeper questions and feel your feelings.

You must make decisions beforehand in order to experience the development and freedom God will bring during an isolation period. First of all decide to stay in isolation until the Lord sovereignly moves you out of isolation. The months seem intensely long for someone in isolation since feelings are experienced on a deep level and since the Lord deals with the soul on a deep level. Like the psalmist in Psalm 13, you will ask "How long O Lord?" over and over again (back to honesty again). There is no real way of telling how long someone may be in isolation—estimates only seem to disappoint. Despite the unpredictability of the length of an isolation experience, you can decide that you will not leave the period until the Lord brings you out of isolation and you can determine proactive steps to reach the heart matters the Lord is wanting to transform in your life.

I have found it helpful when in isolation to belong to a community of people who are committed to me and vice versa. In this supportive context, I commit to making the decision to leave isolation only after we as a group have prayed and discussed together if it is God's timing. I am open to their input in my decision making and I need them to listen to God on my behalf.

Secondly you can determine to go deep with God during an isolation experience. Allow plenty of space in your schedule for personal retreats, overnights at a monastery, long walks in the afternoon, quiet moments after the children are asleep or early morning prayer times. Practice spiritual disciplines such as prayer, solitude, silence, fasting, and meditation (Foster 1988).[23] Many retreat centers offer spiritual direction. Try meeting with a spiritual director for a spiritual check up and for suggestions/disciplines that will move you into deeper relationship with God. Read the Psalms out loud for ten minutes everyday. The Christian church throughout the centuries has used this form of prayer to bring its members into deeper intimacy with the Lord (Peterson 1989: 5 6). Reading the Psalms out loud also uncovers many of the feelings buried in your heart. As you read/speak the feelings of the psalmists you will begin to experience your own feelings. Make sure to journal your prayers thoughts and feelings—this too will help the reflection/spiritual growth process.

Thirdly, knowing that God uses isolation times to transform the character of leaders, take an honest look at your mo-

---

[23] Just as athletes train daily so their muscles respond when needed for a run or for a game, spiritual disciplines exercise the muscles of our spirituality, so we can embrace all of God.

tivations for ministry and any barriers that might keep you from ministering in a healthy way. For example many of the leaders I encounter struggle with drivenness and workaholism. Often performance orientation feeds this drivenness— they must perform, they must succeed in ministry to feel valuable. These patterns may be life long patterns and often it takes the depth of an isolation time to uncover the reasons for the drivenness. In this scenario the process of getting healthy may be accelerated by therapy as well as the development of deep, honest, supportive friendships. For some people the therapy relationship uncovers many of the drivenness patterns as well as the source of drivenness. Barriers can also be healed through inner healing prayer sessions. There are many ways leaders can seek healing and recovery while in isolation. The important idea here is to determine ahead of time to be proactively seeking God and seeking transformation while in isolation. Determine to set goals for personal growth and spirituality while you are in isolation. If you are finding blocks or barriers get prayer and/or counseling to move through these barriers. Be patient isolation—will not last forever.

ISOLATION AND THE TIME-LINE [24]

When Kathy came to Fuller she did not know she would be heading toward a major transition in her life and ministry. She was on a one year furlough with her missions organization and she was eager to return to the field. The Lord's plan however, began to unfold as Kathy began her studies.

In her first class, a leadership development class, Kathy reflected on her life of ministry thus far. With great joy, she realized that God had indeed shaped her and molded her to be a leader. Her ministry experiences came alive as she learned

---

[24] The time-line "is a the linear display along a horizontal axis which is broken up into development phases." (Clinton, "The Time-Line: What It Is and How to Construct It," Altadena: Barnabas Publishers.) The ministry foundation phase incorporates the foundation God has placed in our lives via our upbringing and early ministry formation. It also includes a calling into ministry—leadership transition. The growth phase incorporates the initial period of full-time ministry in which the primary processing objective is to learn ministry by doing ministry. Leaders then transition into competent ministry during which they minister out of their being—who they have been created to be. After this point, they are ready to transition into unique ministry during which leaders' roles fit their unique gifting. When the role, the proper influence, and the gifting match,

the parameters and theory of what she already intuitively knew. Kathy also enrolled in two theology classes. These too were inspiring as Kathy saw God's faithfulness in building his church and as she experienced anew the simplicity and complexity of God's plan in Jesus Christ. As a result of her increasing desire to study, Kathy began to entertain the idea of staying longer at Fuller.

Meanwhile, because of her astuteness in theology, one of Kathy's professors had noticed her work and expressed a desire to mentor her. They began a mentoring relationship immediately, which further allowed Kathy to blossom in her studies. She began to seek God's guidance concerning continued studies. At this point, she was quite certain she would not be returning to the mission field—at least not yet.

After a period of discernment with her support network, Kathy decided to stay at Fuller. However, God's plan for her was not fully revealed until sometime later when she experienced a paradigm shift. Since Kathy had come from a mission board that does not allow women to teach men, the thought had never occurred to her to enter a doctoral program and then return to the mission field to train others for theological education. But, this was exactly what the Lord had in store for her. The professor who had been mentoring Kathy invited her to stay on for further studies. She discovered a particular methodology for training which, if given the proper study and research, could transform ministry in a number of different countries. Kathy went into a discernment process once again and all involved agreed that she should pursue doctoral studies.

Kathy's one year sabbatical turned into a five year doctoral program. When she came to Fuller, she was entering a boundary phase—a transition in her ministry, which propelled her into the next phase of her ministry.

As I have reviewed the case studies of many leaders, I find that a season of isolation often comes when leaders enter boundary phases and during the transition from doing to being.

Boundary Phase[25]

A leader often enters a transition in ministry (a boundary phase) via an isolation experience. No matter how leaders enter isolation, either voluntarily or involuntarily, the isolation time may be the first phase of a transition in leadership which will take them out of their current ministry and lead them into a new ministry God has specifically designed for them. In the figure below, a generic time-line shows the different phases of development in leaders' lives. Normally, leaders experience a significant transition emotionally, spiritually and ministerally as they enter each new phase. Clinton labels these transitions "boundary phases." (Clinton, 1994: 158)

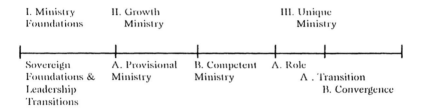

Figure 1. The Basic Ministry Time-Line

These transition periods have several phases which actually coincide with the stages of an isolation period.

The first stage in a boundary time is the entry point. Leaders enter the transition via a precipitating event such as a sabbatical, conflict, or crisis. The entry point may signal the leader's transition out of one role of ministry into another. Leaders may or may not know they will be transitioning into another ministry. If, however, you know that you are in a

---

[25] See Clinton (1992) paper, Boundary Processing, for a detailed explanation of this transition time.

boundary time and that indeed this boundary time will transition you into another ministry, bringing proper closure to your former ministry is a crucial aspect of entering a healthy transition.

Bringing proper closure requires several actions—the most important involves allowing yourself to properly grieve. Depending on the circumstance of the transition, you may be experiencing a lot of feelings as you enter the boundary period. Take time to feel these emotions—anger, sadness, joy—and express them openly with your support network.[26] If you have some control over your departure, ask to have a time in which your church, mission representatives, or support network can send you with their blessing. Have a part in this time in which you can say good-bye and leave your blessing. Write letters of affirmation to those you have worked with.

The second stage of the boundary period involves evaluation. Here, leaders reflect on the ministry they have just left (this stage is similar to the "remembering" of chapter seven). Leaders remember past ministry by drawing out ministry lessons from their experiences and by developing a personal ministry philosophy based on these experiences. While this period can be filled with great joy over what God has accomplished through leaders' lives, it may also be a time of remorse as the mistakes of ministry become apparent. Both the joy and the pain, however, act as catalysts toward deeper understanding of ministry and one's specific contribution to God's Kingdom.

At some point during the second phase of the boundary period, leaders begin to "look up." In other words, they go deeper into relationship with God—many times because this is the only thing they have left to hang on to. As I have referred to earlier in this paper, the leader turns to God for defi-

---

[26] Granger E. Westberg, *Good Grief* (Philadelphia: Fortress Press, 1962). This book briefly describes the ten stages one goes through when grieving a loss. While the book is written for those who have experienced death close to them, it can be used to help leaders maneuver through the loss involved in change.

nition and identity. Going deeper into relationship with the Lord eventually propels the leader into the final stage of the boundary.

The third and final stage of a boundary is the termination stage. During this stage, leaders begin to engage with the future. They explore possibilities for the next stage of development and entertain ideas for future ministry roles. Leaders exiting boundaries usually have many options for future ministry. Therefore, it is important during the boundary/isolation time to reflect on their gifting, and their destiny incidents, as well as the appropriate role for their level of influence. All of these items point the leader toward the appropriate ministry opportunity out of the many options.

Moving From Doing to Being

Jim pursued ministry with great energy and zeal. His passion focused on the lost and he led hundreds to the Lord. Because of his burden for evangelism, Jim planted his first church during his senior year of college. From that point on, he planted a new church every two years. His healing/prayer ministry attracted many, and so Jim often prayed with people late into the night and then he attended early morning prayer meetings with the leaders and church members. When Jim was not training newly converted Christians and leaders, people could usually find him out on the streets sharing the gospel. Jim lived, breathed, ate, drank and slept ministry—practically every hour was filled with some type of ministry event.

The pace, however, was not motivated solely by his love for the lost. Jim found it difficult to be alone, to be left alone with his own thoughts and aspirations. He could not concentrate and often became depressed when he tried to take retreats of silence over a weekend. He did not feel "productive" when he was not engaged in some form of ministry. Jim was primarily motivated by "doing" the ministry—trying the latest church growth technique, trying the latest method for training leaders. In the arena of doing ministry, Jim out did everyone else until finally he became ill.

At first it seemed that Jim had the flu with a sore throat and fever. He did not pay much attention to his illness and pushed on with his ministry. Eventually, the soreness continued until his whole body ached and was fatigued. Jim finally went to the doctor and found that he had mononucleosis. The doctor ordered immediate bed rest.

Being away from ministry sent Jim into a depression which culminated in the Lord revealing to him his drivenness in ministry. The drivenness was not acceptable, for by the time Jim got sick, his relationship with God had been left months ago and he was doing ministry in his own strength.

While the Lord did not make Jim sick, he certainly used the sickness to get Jim's attention and to speak to him about what was motivating his ministry. As Jim reflected during this isolation period, he realized that he had no idea who God had created him to be or what his gifts were. He had very little idea what he wanted out of life. He even wondered if he should be in ministry anymore because he was so driven—could he do ministry from the source of an intimate relationship with God without the drivenness ?

Jim was experiencing an important transition in leadership—moving from a doing base to a being base. Many leaders "do" the tasks of ministry; however, a critical juncture occurs when leaders actually "be" in ministry (Clinton, 1985: 156). In other words, leaders discover and embrace who God has created them to be—as uniquely gifted people with natural abilities, acquired skills and spiritual gifts—and they then function in ministry out of this sense of being. In this light, ministry is only a reflection of the leaders themselves (who the leader is). The activities they choose and the roles they undertake are all appropriate to who God has created them to be. They are not choosing a technique because of the technique, but because it corresponds with who they are as leaders.

God often uses a season of isolation to bring about this transformation because leaders often need to be set aside from the "doingness" of ministry before they can realize how driven they are by it. Thomas Jefferson said, "It is wonderful how much may be done if we are always doing." God, however, has created us with the rhythm of Sabbath rest, and if we lose this rhythm in the midst of doing, we often lose ourselves. In the context of an isolation experience, leaders have the opportunity to ask the deeper questions of what motivates their ministry. Is it success? Is it being recognized by others? Is it somehow meeting their own needs for affirmation and acceptance? They also encounter themselves without a ministry identity and thus wrestle with feeling accepted by God when they are not doing something to "serve" him. During this wrestling, God eventually calls forth and reveals who he has created the leaders to be apart from any ministry or service. In this light, leaders realize that God is thrilled to have a relationship them even if they never were to do any ministry again—God is thrilled with them even if they were never to get out of bed again.

The transformation that emerges in the lives of leaders during a season of isolation allows them a new freedom as they move back into a ministry setting. They are free to take on ministry that truly fits them, and they are free to say no to other opportunities, knowing that they will not "miss out." In their "beingness," they can be free of the compulsion to do more, and they can be free to incorporate quiet reflection and Sabbath into their schedules without needing to attend to the tyranny of the urgent. Leaders ministering out of being are free to calmly move through their ministry schedule, knowing what God has called them to do and what he has not called them to do. Leaders ministering out of being are free.

Reflecting back to the case study on Amy Carmichael, we observe a woman who was truly content to be and not do. As she was too weak to do ministry and could only see a limited number of visitors, Carmichael lived out the remaining years of her life satisfied to spend hours with her Lord. As she lay on her bed and reflected over her life of ministry, and as she entered a deeper level of intimacy with the Lord through her prayer times, Carmichael experienced a creative burst of energy which propelled her writing as never before. She authored some of her greatest and most loved works during this time period; but on a superficial, "doing" level, it seemed that she spent her days wasting away in bed.

While Carmichael's acceptance of her situation did not come without deep questioning of God, her relationship with the Lord was already of such an intimate level that she was able to move through the disappointment of not being able to be active in the daily affairs at the ministry she had founded. The key for working through her struggle was an intimate relationship with God that had been built over many years. This foundation enabled her not to lose heart in the midst of extreme suffering.

Carmichael's example of sweet surrender to the Lord speaks loudly to our achievement oriented Christianity. Her relationship with God was truly enough. Having intimacy with the Lord was her sole joy and crown. Her relationship with God illumines a key insight for those in isolation.

The experience of isolation becomes less daunting in the context of a tried and true intimate relationship with God. If leaders have built into their lives an intimate, daily walk with the Lord, they will experience all their feelings during an isolation period, yet their explicit trust in the Lord under girds and reassures them of God's goodness toward them. They know that the Lord is committed to their lives and to their transformation. and consequently, they can embrace isolation even in the midst of the most intense transitions in ministry .

CONCLUSION

A Season of Isolation—It Will Happen to You, But You Can Be Prepared! It happened in the lives of the leaders in the Bible, it happened in the lives of leaders throughout history and it will happen in your life. Understanding the purpose and process of isolation sheds light on a seemingly dark and confusing period.

You can be prepared for a season of isolation by observing the process in other leaders' lives. Many leaders before you have experienced and moved through a season of isolation. Know that God is faithful to empower your experience of isolation, and he will bring you out of isolation.

You can be prepared for a season of isolation by understanding the process of isolation. Know that as you enter, you will have a sense of being stripped; you will feel insecure as you question who you are. Through this process, the Lord will reveal who he has created you to be, and subsequently, you will experience freedom.

You can be prepared for a season of isolation by trusting that God will transform you. This is God's purpose for you during isolation. God will free you from the things that prevent you from being who you have been created to be. He will woo you into deeper relationship with himself. At the end of isolation, you will like the transformation that God brings to your life.

You can be prepared for a season of isolation by making a decision beforehand to embrace the process of isolation. Make a decision to stay in isolation until the Lord calls you out of it. Make a decision to embrace all that God has for you during isolation. God will do wondrous and amazing things in your life. Expect it and embrace his transformation.

Appendix

Definitions

The Results and Uses of Isolation

Clinton's Seven Steps to Take when Facing Isolation

Refrences Cited

ISOLATION   syn: Setting Aside

Introduction   More than 90% of leaders will face one or more important isolation times in their lives. Most do not negotiate these times very well. Knowing about them and what God can accomplish in them can be a great help to a leader who the faces isolation.

Definition   *Isolation processing* refers to the setting aside of a leader from normal ministry or leadership involvement due to involuntary causes for a period of time sufficient enough to cause and/or allow serious evaluation of life and ministry.

Biblical Examples Job, Jonah, Elijah, Habbakkuk, Paul

Comment   Usually this means that the leader is away from his/her natural context usually for an extended time in order to experience God in a new or deeper way. Sometimes isolation can occur in the ministry context itself.

Comment   Isolation experiences can be short—like intensive times spent away in solitude to meet God or can last up to several months and occasionally more than a year.

Three Major Categories	
Type	Typical Illustration(s)
I. Negative/Sovereign Intervention (Involuntary)	Sickness, war
II. Negative/Opposition (Deserved/self-caused)	Prison, conflict, organizational Discipline
III. Positive Self-Choice	For renewal; for education/renewal

Results or Uses of Isolation

Type	Uses
I. Sovereign Intervention Invountary	• Lesssons of brokenness • Learning about supernatural healing • Lessons about prayer • Deepening of inner life • An intensified sense of urgency to accomplish • Developing of mental facilities • Submission to God • Dependence upon God
II. Negative/Opposition Involuntary	• Lessons of brokenness • Submission to spiritual authority • Value of other perspectives • Dependence upon God
III. Positive/Self-Choice Voluntary	• New perspective on self and ministry • Rekindling of sense of destiny • Get guidance • Open oneself to change • Dependence upon wider body of Christ

Commonalitiies in Most or All Isolation

1. Sense of Rejection (type I or II especially)
2. Sense of Stripping Away – Getting Down to Core Issues (All)
3. Eventually a Deep Need for God (All)
4. Searching for God (All)
5. Submission to God (All)
6. Dependence upon God (All)
7. Rekindling of Desire to Serve God in a Deeper Way (All)

Clinton's 7 Steps To Take In Facing Is

1. Expect it.
About 90-95% of leaders go through an isolatiu.. riod experience of Type I or II.

2. Recognize that there will be a sense of rejection in it.
Because of this it is helpful to keep a log of your divine affirmation and ministry affirmation items. Review them alone with God and feel anew his acceptance.

3. Determine before hand to go deep with God.
He will take you into a place of more dependence, perhaps a place of intimacy that you could not have without this kind of processing.

4. Know that God will indeed meet you in isolation.
Though at first he may appear remote, do not try to move out of isolation on your own until God has met you. Otherwise, you may go through a repeated isolation experience.

5. Know the uses of isolation.
Seek to see and sense which of these God is working into your life.

6. Set goals.
For a Type III isolation experience set goals for personal growth that include dependence, intimacy, and a deeper walk with God.

7. Talk to other Christians who have gone through isolation and other deep processing.
They will give you perspective with a proper empathy.

References Cited

Baldwin, Joyce, G.
1986   *The Message of Genesis 12-50*. Downers Grove: InterVarsity Press.

Bauer, Walter, Gingrich, F. Wilbur, and Danker, Fredrick W.
1979   *A Greek-English Lexicon of the New Testament and Other Early Christian Literature*. Chicago: The University of Chicago Press.

Brother Lawrence
1958   *The Practice of the Presence of God*. Old Tappan, NJ: Fleming H. Revell Co.

Brown, Francis, Driver, S. R., and Briggs, Charles A.
1979   *The New Brown-Driver-Briggs-Gesenius Hebrew and English Lexicon*. Peabody, MA: Hendrickson Publishers.

Bruce, Fredrick F.
1991   *Paul: Apostle of the Heart Set Free*. Grand Rapids: Eerdmans Publishing Co.

Clinton, J. Robert
1989   *Leadership Emergence Theory: A Self-Study Manual for Analyzing the Development of a Christian Leader*. Altadena, CA: Barnabas Pub.

1988   *The Making of a Leader: Recognizing the Lessons and Stages of Leadership Development*. Colorado Springs: Navpress.

1994   *Reader: ML530, Lifelong Development*

Douglas, J. D. ed. et. al.
1982   *The New Bible Dictionary*. Wheaton, IL: Tyndale House Pub., Inc.

Foster, Richard J.
1988   *Celebration of Discipline: The Path to Spiritual Growth*. Revised Ed. San Francisco: Harper & Row.

Kraybill, Donald B.
1978   *The Upside-Down Kingdom*. Scottdale, PA: Herald Press.

La Sor, William S., David A. Hubbard, and Fredric W. Bush,
1982   *Old Testament Survey: The Message, Form, and Background of the Old Testament*. Grand Rapids: Eerdmans Publishing Co.

Perowne, J. J. Stewart
1966   *The Book of Psalms: A New Translation with Introductions and Notes. Vol. 2*. Grand Rapids: Zondervan Publishing Co.

Peterson, Eugene H.
1989   *Answering God: The Psalms as Tools for Prayer*. San Francisco: Harper & Row.

CPSIA information can be obtained
at www.ICGtesting.com
Printed in the USA
LVOW12s0830031017
550545LV00002B/11/P